ECHOES OF SHANNON STREET

The Kidnapping and Murder of Officer Robert S. Hester

James R. Howell

Kelly Nichols
Dana Howell

ISBN: 1470094819
ISBN 13: 9781470094812

sprawled on the concrete still screaming as the monster stood over her roaring.

Her son had stepped out on his porch looking towards his mother's house. The interior of the house was still dark and as he turned to go back inside the horrifying screams coming from down the street reached his ears. He froze as his stilled heart leaped into his throat. He shook off the paralyzing fear, recognizing his mother's voice and ran to the darkened sidewalk and peered towards the plaintiff cries. He saw the large figure standing over the prostrate form crumpled on the sidewalk. He began running along the sidewalk with clenched fists, blood pounding in his ears, deafening the sound of his screams.

"I'm coming MAMA!", "I'm coming!" he bellowed.

The creature's head whipped up catching sight of the muscular figure running towards him. It turned rapidly and began to run along the sidewalk before veering across a front yard. As it got to the drive-way it turned and headed to the short cyclone fence that bordered the backyard and almost made it before tripping over a tricycle. It cursed once as the pain shot through its leg as it jumped up and clambered over the fence and disappeared in the darkness.

The son reached his stricken mother and stared as the beast cut the corner of a house and disappeared from view.

"GREASY-MAN, you motherfucker I'm gonna kill you!" he screeched.

He muttered another curse under his breath while bending down to tend to his mother. He quickly grabbed her outstretched hand and began patting it as he spoke softly to her.

"Mama, are you ok?" he asked.

3

"Y-e-s...baby, your mama's... doing..," she answered in between sobs.

"Can you walk mama?" he asked.

"I,.. believe so... baby, my backside is really hurting me son," she answered quietly.

"Come on mama let me help you up and I'll get you to the house," he whispered, tears streaking his face.

He carefully put his right hand on his mother's arm while he wrapped his left arm around her back and pulled her up. He felt her teeter, almost falling, as she stood unsteadily on her feet, leaning heavily against him. He guided her down the sidewalk towards her house as his mother limped along, moaning softly.

Greasy-man had by now covered five blocks and was hiding in a hedge row gasping for breath while he rubbed his aching knee. He couldn't believe he hadn't seen that fucking tricycle in the backyard. Damn, that hurt he thought as he examined the tear in his navy blue, polyester pants. He slowly made his way between the darkened houses and into the cove. The head lights of the approaching car at first startled him before he recognized the familiar outline atop the roof of the car.

He sat down heavily on the sidewalk, first pulling the gorilla gloves off, before slowly wrenching the gorilla mask from his sweat drenched face. He began unbuttoning the long dark rain coat as the black and white car stopped beside him.

"Well, well, if it isn't the Greasy-man," the chuckling voice said through the open passenger window.

"Yea, well the Greasy-man got his ass whipped by a tricycle," came the reply.

"You always were a clumsy bastard," the driver said laughing, as he climbed out of the car and opened the trunk.

"Fuck, you too," he answered as he walked to the back of the car and tossed the raincoat, mask and gloves in.

He bent down in the trunk and pulled the wide black gun-belt out and began putting it around his waist. The glint of his name tag flashed briefly across his face as the other man turned his flashlight on and began checking the ground to make sure nothing had been dropped on the road or sidewalk.

The two men climbed into the car and as it pulled slowly away from the curb the passenger began describing the latest adventure of the Greasy-man. Both men's laughter spilled out through the open windows of the car as the radio mounted inside crack-led to life.

CHAPTER 2
Siege Underway

The siege - January 1983

Unnamed TACT Officer

I t was pitch black for as far as the eye could see. All the street lights were out and no light shown from any house. The faint outline of the great tree near the little white house was barely discernable. Even its great size was no match for the all enveloping darkness. No cars traveled on the road and no person dared travel on the broken sidewalks. Even the stars had vanished in this black hole. There was no sound other than the occasional shrieking of the frigid January wind.

The dark night coupled with the resounding silence was a forbearance of the evil that had begun to trickle out across the neighborhood and before it ended, the horror that it caused and the misery it did reap would engulf an entire city. And no one would be left untouched.

The shadowy figure atop the school building was unmoving. The mist of his breath floated softly up into the frigid air and was quickly lost in the eight-ball blackness of the sky. The bloodshot eyes stared, transfixed on the darkened house as a tear from his eye slowly trickled along his chapped cheek and onto the hair of his unshaven jaw line.

The screams for help from the little house had stopped many hours ago, thank God, he thought. A shudder ran through his body as the realization of what he was thinking shot through his brain. He hated himself for being so weak and spat on the roof as if this in some way would relieve him of the bitter bile that arose in the back of his throat.

The sounds of violent coughing off to his left echoed into his ears but his eyes never wavered from the target. There was no need to, for the danger he sought was down below him. He wiggled his toes and slowly stamped his feet. He shifted his weight from one foot to the other as his mind drifted off again into the fog of exhaustion.

He watched as a darkened figure crawled slowly between two houses. Barely discernable in the shadows, the figure on the frosted ground stopped and lay motionless. He began to count to himself, as he looked at the still form from the peripheral of his eyes, and as the silent count reached ten, the figure slowly began to slither away into the enveloping shadows of the dark and finally out of the view of his hollowed eyes.

He rubbed his gloved hands together wondering how long it had been since he had felt anything other than a numbed tingling in his fingers. A blast of wind from the north caused his body to quiver uncontrollably and he cursed himself when he could not will his body to stop.

Boots that had once been polished to a mirror shine were now filth covered, with scratches and scraps cris-crossing the dull black exterior.

The sounds of a hoarse cough reached his ears while he answered with his own ragged cough that sounded across the roof, his parched throat burned hot as he stooped at the waist with each spasm and tears of pain welled in his eyes. He detected movement behind him, before he heard the faint shuffle of the footsteps that suddenly stopped.

"Hey, do you need to take five inside?" the ragged voice whispered from the shadows.

"Not yet... go check with the others," he answered.

"You sound like shit, go on down for a few minutes," the voice retorted.

"Fuck you asshole, I ain't done just yet!" he hissed back.

The answer came in the form of muffled footfalls that quickly dissipated.

His gloved hand reached into one of the four pockets of his black jacket pulling out a cough drop, which he quickly popped into his mouth. The burning sensation in his throat suddenly flared up before slowly subsiding.

How many hours had he been here he wondered, how many more hours would pass before he could climb down he thought as he again shifted his weight from one foot to the other. His lower back ached from the continuous angle he had held his body as he tried to avoid showing too much of it above the lip of the building.

His mind drifted off as he stared transfixed at the front of the house. Why and how had things turned out like they had? He didn't know the answer to either and he didn't have the energy to even try and figure it out. He knew one thing. Something was different about this night and this street. Nothing had gone the way it was suppose to. It was as if there was some unforeseen force, some evil, that had taken hold of everyone that had stepped foot on this place.

He had felt the hackles on the back of his neck stand up when he had seen the little house for the first time. A queasiness in his stomach followed by a feeling of gloom had shrouded his entire body. It was as if he had no control over what he did and it seemed that he was in a nightmare that he couldn't awaken from. He had seen it in the eyes of others and though no one mentioned it, he could tell they felt it too.

At the beginning he had felt anger and frustration at the inaction of those in charge. He had muttered uncontrollably as he stewed over what was being done and what should have been done. He had finally lashed out at some of those who carried the burden of responsibility and authority, but who seemed unable to ultimately bear the weight that it bore.

The fire of rebellion had burned out after several hours and though he still harbored feelings of anger he found he could no longer muster the endurance to carry that load and keep his body functioning. It had been too taxing on him. He now merely held his post as he willed his body to remain alert.

There was such a thing as honor, the responsibility to seeing the job through.

"Fucking bullshit," he muttered out loud.

Stop it, stop worrying about shit you can't control, he thought to himself. Do the job, complete the mission and quit your damn bellyaching, his mind told him as his teeth began to chatter. He quickly put his hands over his mouth in an effort to silence the noise.

He began to systematically rub his legs and arms in a vain attempt to stay warm. He knew it was wasted effort but there was nothing else he knew to do unless he went inside to warm up, but he wasn't ready, just yet, to leave his post. Maybe in a few minutes I will, he lied to himself.

He could hear the scrapping of boots behind him on the roof, the boots of men too tired to pick their feet up as they walked. He rubbed his shoulder and as he did so he felt the large white Cobra patch move in unison with his fingers as they dug into his uniform. The back of his gloved hand moved across his chapped cheeks. He lowered his head and closed his eyes, not hearing the shuffling foot falls, as the hushed words floated into his unfeeling ears.

"The Lieutenant told me to relieve you for a little while," the voice said almost pleadingly.

"Come back later," he replied.

"The Lieutenant said either you get off the roof and get warmed up or he is going to personally come up here and kick your ice cold ass," answered the voice.

He closed his eyes as he slowly nodded his head in affirmation of the order. Through half opened eyes he slowly rose in a half crouch, staggering as he headed towards the ladder at the rear of roof. As he stumbled to the ladder he could hear the sound of the pleading voice echoing in his ears.

He wondered if the voice would ever stop calling to him.

CHAPTER 3

The Beginning

January 11ᵗʰ, 1983 - The Beginning

They stood silent in the dark. Great brick and mortar mammoths. Fortresses standing in rows covering three city blocks. Pathways of concrete, like veins of a living creature, ran in and among the structures. Shadows cast by street lights were as silent sentries on the walls.

Hurt Village was one of the largest public housing complexes in a city that had many such teeming developments. The "Hurt's" breadbox shaped buildings were sprawled on the north side of Jackson Avenue. Streets running north and south bordered and slashed through the complex.

Nearby stood a grocery store frequented by the people of the Village. An island just a sliver, of black top and commerce, surrounded by Jackson Avenue and North Parkway. The bright lights stood in stark contrast to the darkened walls of Hurt Village.

The Kroger store stood on a finger shaped strip of land between two of the most heavily traveled roadways in Memphis. A small street named Peyton connecting Jackson and North Parkway ran in front of the store. Peyton completed the total encirclement of the store and its parking lot. The numbers 544 were above the doors.

Business was always good and the store had thrived since opening, despite minor thefts of merchandise from the store, or an occasional car stolen from the parking lot or even, once in a blue moon, the robbery of a customer on the property.

Kroger had hired off duty Memphis police officers to work as security guards. They ranged throughout the store and walked the parking lot, continuously on the lookout for the drunks and beggars that congregated around the store.

Bill's Twilight Lounge was just up the street and always hopping on the weekends. No one could say for sure what its hours of business were for the establishment. The simple fact was it never seemed to close. Inebriated customers, from the lounge, would often stagger into Kroger's to buy that gallon of milk they had been sent out to get two hours early.

The front glass door of the lounge was painted over, with iron bars covering the inside and outside of the door. The windowless tavern, as officers who worked the area well knew, had been the site of more than one alcohol related shooting or stabbing.

At around 8:00pm on Tuesday night, January 11th, Memphis police officer Don Ross was working security for the store. Business had been steady, and he had checked the parking lots but had little real concern that anyone would be loitering outside in the near freezing weather that Memphis was suffering through. Ross had walked the aisles of the store looking for anyone who might decide that tonight was "five finger discount" night at Kroger.

Tona Smith was tired. She had just finished her shift at the store and couldn't wait to get home. Her feet were hurting from standing almost the whole day.

She dreaded having to go outside and face that north wind that she just knew would be whipping across the parking lot.

As she prepared to sign out she laid her purse down on the counter. She turned away, signed out and turned back to pick up her purse. It was gone from the counter.

"Damn!" Smith muttered under her breath.

Where had her purse gone? She couldn't believe her luck. She just wanted to leave and now some low down person had snatched her purse up. Smith reported the theft to the manager and Ross. At 8:26pm Smith called the West Precinct telling the officer that her purse had been stolen.

At 8:30pm, a west precinct car was dispatched. Officers Kirk Renfro and Voretta Mhoon, car 435, arrived at the scene at 8:39pm. Mhoon took Smith's information for the report. Ross exchanged pleasantries with the two officers and then briefed them as to what had happened.

Ross had seen two male blacks leave the store with the purse. The taller of the two looked like a student he had taught at Manassas High School a few years earlier but he couldn't remember his name. He had described the young man to an employee who had said that sounded like Michael Coleman. The employee also told Ross that Coleman lived with his mother in Hurt Village. Mhoon wrote down the description of Coleman: 6'2, 245lbs, 18 years old, home address 630 North Seventh, Apt. A.

Ross, along with Renfro and Mhoon, left the Kroger store and made the two minute drive on Jackson Avenue to the far western edge of Hurt Village. Mhoon slowed the car after turning right and going north on Seventh Street.

All three commented about how deserted the Village looked. During warmer weather the sidewalks and open stairwells would have been packed with people. The three laughed in unison when it was mentioned that maybe the cold weather had something to do with it.

The beam from the car mounted spotlight illuminated the foot high numbers affixed to the brown brick walls, as Mhoon strained looking for numbers 630. When the building was located, Mhoon steered the black and white cruiser over the curb and parked it, engine running, on the sidewalk. She wanted to get closer to the building but didn't want to get a complaint about parking on the grass. The officers climbed out of the cruiser, Mhoon opening the back door for Ross. The officers pulled their collars up around their necks as they hurriedly walked towards apartment A.

They knocked on the door and were let in by a middle aged, woman who identified herself as Betty Greer Coleman, Michael Coleman's mother.

As the officers entered the sparse two-story, four room apartment they glanced at the three men sitting inside. Ms. Coleman was told by the officers that her son, Michael, was suspected of taking a woman's purse from the Kroger Store and they needed to talk to him. Betty told the officers that she hadn't seen her son since yesterday.

Officers wrote down information as Betty confirmed her son's age as 18 years old. Betty told the officers that Michael had been in some trouble with the police before and went on to say that Michael had been to Juvenile Court on more than one occasion. Officers further learned that Michael was unemployed, but Betty added that Michael had gotten his high school diploma.

When asked who the other young men were in the apartment, Betty told the officers that they were three of her five sons. She mentioned that Michael might be over at Berg's house, off Hollywood, in Hyde Park. Her son, Ben, picked up the phone and placed a phone call. He spoke for a few seconds.

"The police are over here looking for Michael. They say he stole a purse from Kroger," Ben said into the phone. He then handed the phone to Ross.

Ross took the phone and heard a male voice.

"What the fuck you talking about, Michael ain't stole no mother fucking purse!" the male said.

"I want to speak to Michael," Ross replied.

Ross heard the man telling Michael to come to the phone.

"What's going on Michael?" Ross said. "This is Don Ross from Kroger, do you remember me?"

"I don't know what you're talking about, I ain't been to no Kroger," Michael said.

"Where are you? Give me the address and phone number where you're at," Ross said.

"Man, I ain't stole no Goddam purse; I don't know what you're fucking talking about!" Michael screamed.

Ross hung up the phone immediately.

After telling Betty that her son needed to come talk to the police, the three officers left the apartment.

When officers arrived back at the store, Smith was given the bad news. They had not found her purse or the man they suspected of taking it. Smith was told that it was doubtful her purse would be found. Officers told Smith that an investigator would call her in a few days and that an arrest warrant could be obtained for Coleman, if it turned out, he had taken the purse.

The two officers retreated to their car, waving to Ross, as they left. Renfro and Mhoon sat in the car but didn't immediately pull away from the store. They looked over the report, making sure they had all the necessary information.

At 9:00pm the Dodge Polaris police car pulled slowly away from the curb. Renfro and Mhoon quickly forgot about the stolen purse. It had been a wild goose chase going over talking to mama. Hell, Coleman wasn't even the right kid. The theft of a purse was not worth worrying about. The officers headed off to get coffee. Neither officer complained. They both knew the

17

weekend would be here soon enough and they would be humping calls all night.

Betty Greer Coleman looked out the window, watching the three officer's trudge back to their car. She couldn't imagine what Michael was thinking, taking a woman's purse. She just didn't know what had gotten into him lately.

Betty thought back to yesterday's conversation with her son. Michael had come home, telling her he had been fasting for three days, at Berg's house in Hyde Park. Coleman told his mother that the world was going to end and these were the latter days. She tried to talk some sense into him, but Michael had just kept on rattling off at the mouth.

She wondered where her child's mind had gone to and where he was getting these crazy thoughts. Should she have told the officers about her conversation with Michael? The officers wouldn't care and she sure didn't think it was any of their business anyway. But he was sure spending a lot a time over in Hyde Park. She knew that several of the young men from Hurt Village had also been staying over at Berg's house.

As Betty turned away from the window she glanced over at Ben, as her thoughts drifted to other matters. Suddenly the phone rang. Her son Ben answered it, then held it out.

"Mama, it's Michael," Ben said.

Betty walked to get the phone from her son.

"Mama, are the police still there?" Michael asked.

"No, Michael, they just left. Did you steal that purse?" Betty asked.

"No! I didn't take no purse," Michael answered.

The conversation lasted for several more minutes before Michael got ready to hang the phone up.

"Bye Mama," Michael said.

"Bye, baby," Betty answered.

As she hung up the phone she remembered something else that Michael had said to her yesterday. She thought for a moment, this is January 11th, then it came to her.

Something Michael had said...

Michael had warned his mother to prepare herself.

Prepare myself, she thought.

Prepare myself for what?

CHAPTER 4
A Stolen Purse

The sound was unmistakable. To anyone new to the area of the Hyde Park community, the sound was not unlike two busted chainsaws. They both cranked up with loud roars, then died down, idled and finally quit. Each successive crank garnered the same results.

To the residents that lived in and around Hollywood Street and Chelsea Avenue, there was no doubt who was fussing. Two chainsaws would have been no less bothersome but definitely not as entertaining. The hoarse, gruff, voices of old man Albert and crazy George Lincoln* serenaded those within earshot. Albert and Lincoln were just two of the many residents that gave the Hyde Park community its individuality, that made it different from the other communities that together formed Memphis.

There were dozens upon dozens of these little communities within Memphis each as different and independent as any like number of small towns and cities which stretched across the state. To the residents that lived within these Memphis communities - Orange Mound, Knob Hill, Frayser, Springdale and Bunker Hill - their neighborhood always came first.

The residents were fiercely proud of their individual communities and suspicious of outsiders. The surrounding streets were not simply paths for cars. They were boundaries that defined those neighborhoods and the people in them. Crossing a street, from one community to another, could be considered a border incursion and in some cases, considered tantamount to a full scale invasion.

Hyde Park was one of these communities. It was situated in north Memphis, its epicenter being the Hollywood and Chelsea intersection. There was the funeral home and just a little west of that, a gas station owned by a man named Mose. Across the street, Old William ran a beer joint with rooms for rent above the bar. Wong's Grocery was at the northwest corner of Hyde Park Street and Chelsea. It was a small, red, brick building with an awning over the front.

The Wong's, Shang Foo and Kammoi, along with their five children, had come to Memphis from Hong Kong several years before. Soon they had two small grocery stores operating in Memphis. The father and several of his children operated their store on Farrington, in south Memphis, while the mother and the other children ran the north Memphis store.

Old Man Albert was a regular there. Davey Mackins* would chose the sidewalk, in front of Wong's, to stick a knife in a white boy named Randy. Shakey Jones*, who some residents said was a dope dealer and thief, could be found further down Chelsea hanging out near Sim's barbershop. Crazy George Lincoln was constantly wandering the streets. It was rare to see him without a brick or rock in his hand. Lincoln had a trigger finger and would hurl his missile at anyone who rubbed him the wrong way.

Further north up Hyde Park, near the little street of Boxwood, crack cocaine would make the area infamous in the mid-eighties. But that was in the future, and in 1983, the area consisted of older, houses in a quiet working class neighborhood.

There was an Elementary School in the neighborhood. Shannon Elementary sat on the north side of a street that bore its name. Shannon was a short street, with small framed houses and neatly cut yards. These same yards were now worn by winter, but in the spring, would bloom with pink snapdragons, the purple hue of the lilies and a lush canopy of green leaves from trees that lined both sides of the roadway.

Across the street from the school in the yard at 2239 Shannon stood the largest tree on the street. The great oak provided shade to the forty-three year old house. It was a deceivingly large house, with white wood on the exterior, and a contrasting light grey roof.

The owners of the house were Lindberg and Dorothy Sanders. The 5'9 Sanders, who had begun sporting a beard, was originally from Drew, Mississippi. He developed his skill with hammer, nails and mortar in Mississippi and made a living doing carpentry and concrete work after moving to Memphis. Sanders had helped pour concrete during the construction of the Raleigh-Springs Mall in the seventies.

Friends of Sanders' children remembered parties that Sanders and his wife Dorothy threw for their kids. The Sanders' house had been a gathering place for the teenagers, who had marveled at the interior decor, which included a sunken den, a large aquarium and a flowing fountain, all of which Sander's himself had built. It had been considered, by some, the nicest house in the neighborhood.

On that cold Tuesday evening of January 11th, a visitor was coming to 2239 Shannon. The headlights from his car momentarily lit up the great oak. The '73 Lincoln slowed to an almost complete stop as the driver debated on where to park. The decision was made as the big, yellow Continental came to a stop, with its wheels resting several feet off the curb, in the circular drive in front of the school.

David Lee Jordan, Sr. locked the car and quickly walked across Shannon, and into the yard. He passed under the great oak, by two rusty lawn chairs that stood ignored in the cold weather, and stepped on to the covered porch. He entered the house without knocking.

Years had passed since kids had dominated the house, but it was still a place for people to gather. Jordan was one of those people, now part of an older crowd that met regularly there to smoke reefer and listen to Lindberg preach.

As Jordan stepped inside, he greeted others that were already there. Directly in front of him was Larnell Sanders, the twenty seven year old son of Lindberg. He was standing by the fireplace, talking to his father and Michael Coleman. Over and surrounding the fireplace was a mantel, with a picture of a smiling couple flanked by two decorative wine bottles.

Looking to his right, Jordan waved a hello at Cassell Harris and Earl Thomas who were on the couch in the living room, talking with Andrew "JuJu" Houston, seated on the love seat. Other men moved about the house with the familiarity that had come from many past visits, visits that for this group were frequent and informal.

After closing the front door, Jordan turned to his immediate left and entered through a doorway, tossing his black, waist-length jacket on the queen-size bed. He left the bedroom through a second doorway that lead directly into the kitchen. As he passed through the kitchen he glanced out the window, just glimpsing the far eastern corner of the school. Jordan found a brown metal folding chair leaning against the wall of the den. He sat down heavily and leaned his back against the east wall of the house and closed his eyes.

Someone coming in the back door momentarily startled Jordan from his nap. His eyes shifted to the left, and through the second of three doorways that led off the den he saw "Skinny" McCray standing in the sunken meeting room, holding the back door open for Thomas Smith. Jordan closed his eyes again. It would be a few minutes before Lindberg started preaching and a short nap wouldn't hurt.

These thirteen men who came to hear Lindberg shared many similarities. They were young, black, for the most part uneducated, and highly impressionable. Many were from Hurt Village.

The group had no formal name but some of the members called themselves the Lunch Bunch, because so many people in the neighborhood said the whole group was crazy or out to lunch. Lindberg preached from the Old Testament while the members drank wine and smoked marijuana (a herb of the earth and as such a gift from God). They spent long hours in the large, open meeting room at the back of the house, debating and discussing topics Lindberg chose. The past days had been filled less with debate, and more on preparation for something far more serious. Lindberg had prophesied the end of the world would come on Monday, January 10th, 1983.

In his prophecy, the moon would turn crimson and blood would drip down to earth. In his emotional sermons, Lindberg had foretold of the moon coming down to earth and all those who did not follow his words would burn to death. Recently, Lindberg had ordered his followers to begin fasting and for the last three days, the group had consumed little more than wine and marijuana.

Some people called the group a cult. It was later said that Lindberg was practicing mind control. Some members of the group would admit they referred to Lindberg as Little Jesus.

Others said the group got together just to smoke pot and get liquored up. They pointed out that, since Dorothy and her daughter were no longer living at the house, Lin and his bunch were just getting down and getting funky.

On January 11th, Lindberg was teaching a new psalm to the group who were all sitting in the living room when he was interrupted by the ringing of the phone. He walked over, picking it up.

"What?" Lindberg answered.

"Berg, this is Ben, The police are over here looking for Michael. They say he stole a purse from Kroger," Ben said.

Before Lindberg could say anything, he heard a voice he didn't recognize on the phone.

"What the fuck you talking about, Michael ain't stole no mother fucking purse!" Lindberg shouted.

"I want to speak to Michael," the voice said.

"Michael," Lindberg said. "Come talk to this motherfucker on the phone says you stole a purse."

Coleman walked across the room and took the brown phone from Lindberg.

"Hello," Coleman said.

"What's going on Michael? This is Don Ross from Kroger, do you remember me?" Ross asked.

"I don't know what you're talking about. I ain't been to no Kroger," Coleman said.

"Where are you? Give me the address and phone number where you're at?" Ross asked.

"Man, I ain't stole no Goddam purse! I don't know what you're fucking talking about!" Coleman screamed. He realized Ross had hung up the phone as he slammed the received down.

"Why did you hang the phone up?" Lindberg asked.

"I didn't, the cop hung up first," Coleman replied.

"That's a lie. You shouldn't have hung up, you got nothing to hide," Lindberg said.

"I didn't hang up first he did," Coleman answered back.

"Don't you know it makes you look like you did something when you do that," Lindberg said.

"I didn't hang up first," Coleman said.

"You call those folks back and tell them where you're at," Lindberg ordered, his piercing dark eyes flashing as he spoke.

Coleman picked up the phone.

"Ben, let me speak to mama," Coleman said. He waited a moment, picking at his white V-neck sweater. "Mama, are the police still there?" Coleman asked.

"No, they just left, did you steal that purse?" Betty asked.

"No, I didn't take no purse," Coleman said. He spoke for several more minutes before he hung up the phone.

Lindberg then told Coleman to pick up the phone and call the police. Coleman was confused as to why he would want to call the police and for that matter, what he would say when he did.

"You call them and tell them where you're at. You ain't done nothing wrong," Lindberg said.

Michael dialed the phone and listened as it rang. The time was 8:58pm.

Police Call Taker Scarbrough: - **Police and Fire**
Coleman: - **Hello, this is uh,.... Michael Coleman...uh**
(Several seconds of silence)
Scarbrough: - **Ok, what do you want?**

Memphis police call taker, D. A. Scarbrough, listened to the caller. In the background Scarbrough could hear a male voice cursing and coaching Coleman on what to say.

Coleman: - **What.......**
Scarbrough: - **Uh.**

Coleman: - **This is... this is Michael Coleman, did you'all have a call... down there on me?**

Scarbrough: - **I don't know, where was you....**

Coleman: - **A warrant?**

Scarbrough: - **Uh, a warrant?**

Coleman: - **Down to come by my house about me stealing something or something.**

Scarbrough: - **When?**

Coleman: - **A pocketbook.**

Scarbrough: - **When?**

Coleman: - *Today.*

Scarbrough: - **When was they by there?**

Coleman: - **About,.. about five minutes ago.**

Scarbrough: - **Where are you at?**

Coleman: - **I'm at...** (voice in background saying 2239 Shannon)**...2239 Shannon.**

Scarbrough: - **2239, what?**

Coleman: - **Shannon.**

Scarbrough: - **Shannon?**

Coleman: - **Yea...** (voice in background saying in Hollywood)**... in Hollywood.**

Scarbrough: - **Where did they go by and look for you at... over there on Shannon?**

Coleman: - **Yea.**

Scarbrough: - **... I'll check with them and have them come back over there... Ok?**

Coleman: - **Yea.**

Scarbrough: - **Ok.**

   —Line disconnected—

Scarbrough made an inter-office call to the dispatcher handling the North Precinct.

Scarbrough: - **Oh, did you have somebody looking for somebody on Shannon?**
North Dispatcher Jim Wiechert: - **Not that I know of.**
Scarbrough: - **He said police were there looking for him on some kinda of purse snatch and he's back over there on Shannon...**

Dispatcher Wiechert: - **Uh, must have been day shift. We haven't been over there all day.**
Scarbrough: - **Alright, I'll send you a ticket on it.**

Coleman had hung the phone up, then went and sat on the couch. Lindberg paced about the room speaking to the entire group.

T.C., Earl, Coleman and Jordan were sitting on the couch on the north wall. Pete, Tyrone, Jackie and Reginald were on the love seat against the west wall. Larnell, JuJu, and Cassell were seated on the couch against the south wall. Joe was standing near the hallway door by Fred, who was sitting on the floor.

Lindberg had always preached about the group being one. He had told them on numerous occasions that he had died once and could never die again. Only God could kill him. If the group stayed together then no harm could come to any of them.

"Some of you are going to get somewhere when the police get here, cause you're scared." Lindberg said.

CHAPTER 5
Schwill and Hester

The light brown, brick building, with the tinted windows, was nestled among the trees. If not for its size, some driving north on Allen from Frayser Boulevard, might have failed to see it.

The building's address was 3633 Allen. A drive-way led from Allen around the south side of the building. Behind the building was an enormous parking lot, complete with a set of gas pumps and a two bay garage.

The building was not old, but, in fact was still in its infancy. It was never closed for business and its occupants were always on the job.

The evening routine had begun as it always did. Starting at 3:30pm, they began to arrive. At first it was one or two at a time. As 3:45pm came around, the number coming in was three or four at a time. By 3:55pm, one or two more would file in.

The room where these twenty-five to thirty men and women congregated every day was now alive with the usual banter and loud laughter. Good natured insults and obscenities were tossed to and fro.

As was their nature, the people gathering here each evening, could be found sitting in the same area of the room, if not their same seat. There was another reason for the seating arrangement that others probably would not understand.

As the four men stepped into the room everyone stopped talking, and rose from their seats. Each put on their hat and waited for their name to be called.

After hearing their name called, each was told where their area of responsibility would be for the evening. It was not as if it was a big secret. The people in this room knew where they would be living their life, for five days each week, eight hours a day. But the ritual had to be honored and everyone present understood that.

One man, a Lieutenant, spoke to the assembled crowd, as the other three men, two Lieutenants and a Captain, stood off to the side. This one man read from a stack of papers that he had placed on the wooden podium in front of him. He didn't bother to read every word on every paper. His job was to inform those gathered, not bore them.

The read-out board, which was actually a clip board, contained memos, broadcasts on wanted persons, additional patrols (locations to be checked throughout the shift), death notices and other paperwork that covered a wide variety of topics.

The meeting or roll call ended by 4:25pm. The loud, rough language and laughter began immediately. The officers filed out the door and into the large, rear parking lot. They loaded up their cars and filled them with gas. The parking lot, would be deserted and quiet, once again, by 4:50pm.

The cars had driven out, in a line, like soldiers on the march or maybe toy soldiers on an assembly line. When the cars reached Allen Street, each one turned right and came to a stop at the intersection of Allen and Frayser. From this intersection, the cars began to separate in different directions.

It was like this every night. These men and women shared twenty or thirty minutes together. These minutes were shared without the glare of blue lights, the wail of sirens or the presence of strangers.

Officers Robert Hester and Ray Schwill were two of those people. They both had attended roll call that night. They had sat together, as they did each night, as the Lieutenant called each officer's name. They sat together because that's what partners did. Each officer in that roll call sat with the person whose life they would depend on, for the next eight hours. No one chose their seat according to race or sex.

It would not always be that way. Times would change and so would the officers who would choose to wear the uniform. But this was 1983 and loyalty to your partner and to your shift still mattered.

Both officers worked the "Charlie" shift at the North Precinct. The North Precinct, like the other three precincts, was subdivided into wards. The ward Hester and Schwill rode in was designated 128. This small ward included the Hyde Park area.

Hester and Schwill had filed out of the building with everyone else. They were two very different men, yet so much alike. Bobby was quiet and reserved Ray talkative and outgoing. Hester was several inches shorter and pounds lighter than Schwill's six foot, two hundred pound frame.

Both played on the precinct softball team.

Hester rarely came to any parties held by the police. He instead chose to spend quiet time with his wife, Anita. Schwill was the life of the party. Hester was known to tell a few jokes and trade an insult or two. Schwill had a million jokes and was not shy about telling them all.

Hester didn't waste his words, and his voice, even when raised, rarely offended. Schwill talked loud and often. The projection in his voice was sometimes misunderstood by those who did not know him.

The two had been partners for almost a year and both shared a love for the job.

After leaving the precinct Schwill turned west on to Frayser, as he and Hester talked about what to eat. Both wanted to get something in case it got busy later. As Schwill drove, the smoke from his cigarette, curled into the air. Hester, riding shotgun, leaned back and laughed as Schwill finished the punch line to a joke.

A short time later Schwill turned off Frayser on to Rangeline and negotiated the car into a parking space, at the Souther Kitchen. The partners got out and eased into the eatery.

They found a table and exchanged the usual round of hello and how are you with the employees and familiar customers. The officers had eaten quite a few meals here, so they were well known to the staff.

At the table near them, Ed Harker, an off duty Sergeant with the department, sat eating his dinner. The three socialized as Hester and Schwill waited on their food.

With their dinner consumed, Schwill had smoked a cigarette and Hester had eaten a piece of coconut cream pie. Harker mentioned to Schwill and Hester that he had quit smoking and was on a diet. Schwill and Hester had both gotten a laugh out of Harker's double confession.

After leaving the diner, the officers handled alarm calls to 3998 Wales and 1337 Warford. They spoke with a Ms. Williams at 2327 Vandale about some suspicious persons in a field near her house. Williams later remembered that the officer that drove did all the talking. The other officer, she remembered, didn't say anything and had stood off to the side.

Around 6:45pm they made a suspicious person call at 2138 Chelsea where they spoke with the employees for several minutes before getting a mental case call at 1643 N. Barksdale at approximately 6:52pm. After clearing the Barksdale call Schwill and Hester answered three more alarm calls within forty-five minutes.

Sometime around 8:00pm they drank coffee with one of the shift Lieutenants, R. B. Summers, at Jackson and Hollywood.

Just before 9:00pm, Hester and Schwill stopped in at the Drive-In Grocery at 2138 Chelsea and stood talking to the employees. They had made an earlier call in regards to male hanging out near the rear of the business.

It had been an uneventful night. Their call load had been somewhat steady, with nine calls on their log sheet. At 9:00pm, two hours until the end of shift, another call came over their radios.

Dispatcher: - **128, a.. complaint at 2239 Shannon, a male named Coleman advised he just arrived home and neighbors said the police were looking for him earlier in regards to some purse snatch, he's there, he wants to try and get it straightened out. As far as we know it was on day shift, we have no calls on it ourselves, 2239 Shannon.**

As Hester wrote the address down in the palm of his hand, Schwill keyed up the mike on his portable radio, and acknowledge the call.

Schwill: - **28.**

It was just another call, like so many others, that these two officers had made over the years. The partners said goodbye to the employees and walked out to their car.

As Schwill got behind the wheel, Hester wrote down the address on the log sheet, along with the call time.

Schwill pulled out into traffic on Chelsea. Both officers glanced, at One Leg Luke, limping by on the sidewalk. The police cruiser passed by Wong's Grocery, as Schwill made the left hand turn, to go north on Hyde Park.

The partners shared a few moments of conversation about the call and what they might do after work. Hester, the quiet, former Army M.P. from Sheffield, Alabama, laughed as Schwill cracked another joke. Schwill turned on to Shannon as Hester thought again about moving him and his wife back to Alabama and maybe getting a job with TVA.

He had never planned on being a police officer.

CHAPTER 6

Arrival at House

Car 128: - **28 scene.**
Dispatcher: - **128 scene.**

S chwill parked in front of the house, leaving the headlights on and the engine and heater running. The partners walked across the yard towards the house, their breath turning to white mist in the cold dry air. Hester looked to his right at a late model, grey, Continental sitting in the drive-way. Both officers looked up at the American Flag, hanging from the flag pole, attached to the side of the house, near the front porch.

Wind chimes, suspended from the front porch, and pushed by the breeze, were plinking a song, to the two veteran officers. The partners stepped to the front door and stood almost shoulder to shoulder, under the overhang of the porch which was steadied by wrought iron supports. Schwill ducked his head, narrowly avoiding bumping into one of the two hanging plants. Both officers quickly glanced at the windows on either side of the porch.

Schwill knocked on the door and identified himself. From within the house, a male voice yelled to the officers to come in. The officers opened the door and stepped into the living room and out of the cold.

Hester and Schwill stood for a moment inside the door, as they quickly glanced around. To the right of the fireplace, Schwill saw a doorway that opened to a short hallway that ran into what appeared to be a bathroom. As he continued scanning right, Schwill saw several male blacks sitting down. One of the men, who was holding a brown phone in his hand, stood up.

"What do you want?" he asked.

Schwill judged the man to be in his mid to late forties; about five foot seven, with a beard. Schwill would later learn that the man's name was Lindberg Sanders.

As Schwill tried to explain why they were there, Lindberg interrupted him in mid sentence. Schwill stepped across the room, near the fireplace, stopping within a few steps of Lindberg.

"Did you call us?" Schwill asked.

"Didn't you call us?" Lindberg asked.

"If you don't need us then we'll leave," Schwill answered.

Lindberg shrugged his shoulders as he lazily pointed at a teenager who got up from the couch and walked over to the officers.

"That's him," Lindberg said.

The officers looked at the teen, who would be later identified as Michael Coleman. Coleman fists were balled up, his chest heaving, his eyes glaring. He was giving the officers a look that Schwill would later describe as menacing.

"Do you know anything about a stolen purse?" Schwill asked Coleman.

"I don't know a mother fucking thing, about a purse snatch!" Coleman yelled.

Lindberg suddenly starting ranting and cursing at the officers, too.

Schwill looked over at the twelve other men who were still seated quietly. The men seemed oblivious to what was going on and would not look directly at either officer. Instead, they cut their eyes at each other. Schwill noticed that several of the men were sitting on the edge of their seats. Lindberg continued ranting, still clutching the phone.

"I didn't steal no fucking purse!" Coleman said.

Still the men continued to sit.

The two officers glanced at each other as Schwill began reaching for his portable radio. Both officers knew something was wrong.

Schwill keyed up his radio and calmly spoke into it.

Schwill: - **128, start us another car over here**.
Dispatcher: - **Ok 128; 129, at 2239 Shannon, back up 128, possible wanted party, 2239 Shannon.**
Car 129: - **29.**
Car 159: - **59, disregard my special, show me in route to meet-em.**
Car 147: - **147, do you want me to pull down that way?**
Dispatcher: - **Ok, 147.**

Lindberg's voice became louder.

"We can get this all worked out if you and Coleman will just step outside with us," Schwill said.

Where it's safe, Schwill didn't dare add.

Lindberg asked Schwill several questions in rapid fire succession. Schwill tried to answer each question, but Lindberg suddenly went onto something else.

"Do you know Jesus?" Lindberg asked.

"I do," Schwill replied. "How bout you, do you know Jesus?"

"Yes, but why won't you answer my questions?" Sanders hissed. "Why won't you answer my questions?"

"I'm trying to..." Schwill replied.

"Why won't you answer my questions?"

"If you..." Schwill tried to answer.

"Why won't you answer my questions?"

Schwill was unable to say a word as Lindberg repeated the question over and over again. Coleman began to pant louder as Hester moved up, in an effort to calm the six foot Coleman down.

"You both need to come outside," said Schwill sternly.

"I ain't going fucking nowhere!" screamed Coleman.

Schwill, along with Hester, began to slowly back up towards the door. Seeing the officers inching backwards, Lindberg and Coleman bellowed in unison.

"Neither of you are going no fucking where!"

Coleman stepped towards the officers and landed a clenched fist to the side of Schwill's head, then stepped backed near Lindberg. Both officers continued moving backwards knowing they had to get outside. Coleman moved towards the officers again.

"You ain't going nowhere!" Coleman said, as he tried to grab Schwill.

Schwill and Hester grabbed the large teen, and started to drag him from the house. He bucked against them, struggling.

They had Coleman to the front porch, when they heard the shouted command.

"Get'em!" Lindberg said.

All the males sitting down in the living room rushed towards Schwill and Hester. Still struggling with Coleman, Schwill grabbed his radio and yelled into it,

Schwill: - **128, HELP!!!**

Dispatcher: - **128 is calling for assistance! 128 is calling for assistance! 2239 Shannon, Ok 147.**

Car 147: - **Check.**

Dispatcher: - **129!**

Car 129: - **Ok 29, give us a location.**
Car 156: - **56, show me pulling down.**

It was now no longer business as usual. It was very rare to hear any officer call for help. Even more so when it was a two man car. Cars in the North Precinct were now barreling towards Shannon Street, blue lights on and sirens wailing.

A few cars had to ask for a location (directions to the address).

Dispatcher: - **gonna run east,....it's gonna run back,....off of,.....2200 block is gonna be just west of Boxwood. Go west on Heard from Hollywood or you can go north on Hyde Park from Chelsea and run into the 2200 block of Shannon....**

None of the officers would arrive in time to see the fight taking place on the porch and front yard.

Still holding his portable radio, Schwill watched as the men rushing towards him seemed to be moving in slow motion. He glanced towards Hester, who was fighting with Coleman, but could not hear the sounds of their struggle. Schwill looked back towards the front door, just as several blurred shapes impacted into him.

Schwill felt his body flying through the air as the sheer weight and force of the impact sent him cart wheeling off the porch. With the wind knocked out of him, Schwill looked towards the porch, again trying to catch sight of his partner. He recognized Hester's silhouette pinned against the front door under a wave of bodies.

Schwill was struggling to get up when Lindberg, Coleman, and another male jumped on top of him, and immediately began hitting him in the head and face, with their fists. Coleman then quickly stood up and began kicking Schwill in the head repeatedly.

Schwill could hear Hester screaming. "Ray come get me! Come help me, Ray, they've got me!"

Still on his back, Schwill saw only bluish-white stars exploding in front of his eyes. Pain shot through his head. He was trying to ward off the blows to his face with his left hand as he clawed to get to his pistol free from his holster.

Schwill felt the over-sized wooden grips of his pistol and began to wrap his fingers around it as his thumb simultaneously unsnapped the thumb-break, pancake style holster. One of the men screamed out a warning as Lindberg and Coleman grabbed Schwill's hand and pistol.

Schwill squeezed his right hand even tighter around the grips, grabbing the barrel with his left hand, trying to wrench it free. He felt himself grower weaker and willed himself to remain conscious. As darkness began enveloping his brain, Schwill desperately tried to get his finger on the trigger. But he started drifting away into unconsciousness and he felt the pistol slipping from his hands. Lindberg pulled the pistol free as the streak of orange-yellow flame erupted from his gun and the echoes of the shot rang in his ears.

He caught a glimpse of then lost sight of Hester's limp form being half-dragged, half-carried into a room by the front door.

Schwill's relief at not being hit by the bullet was quickly replaced by fear, as he felt himself being picked up. He stared up at the blur of stars set in the clear sky. He felt pain shoot through his back as he was thrown on the carpeted floor in the northwest corner of the living room.

Another quick blur of a chandelier hanging from the ceiling, then it was blocked out by the two men who stepped up and stood over him. Lindberg began asking Schwill about Jesus and God as Schwill painfully turned his head to face him. Lindberg was pointing the pistol at him, the muzzle only inches from his head.

Schwill could tell from Lindberg's movements that the bullet fired outside had not hit him either.

"Why do you want to kill me?" Schwill asked.

Lindberg's reply was so incoherent that Schwill couldn't understand it. He saw the two males that had been standing over him leave the room. He was now alone with Lindberg, and he knew this was his only chance. He raised his hands in the surrender position just as Lindberg again put the pistol to Schwill's head.

Schwill grabbed the pistol, pulling Lindberg down to the floor, both of them rolling across the floor, fighting for the gun.

The much larger Schwill quickly began to gain control of the weapon. Lindberg screeched for help. Seconds later, two men were in the room, kicking and punching Schwill. Lindberg managed to again wrench the pistol free, and he leaned in Schwill's face, cursing loudly, the barrel of the gun pressed to Schwill's temple.

"Please don't kill me," Schwill pleaded.

Lindberg moved to within inches of Schwill's face, spittle from his hissed threats sprinkling Schwill's face. Schwill watched wide-eyed as Lindberg began pulling back on the trigger. The cylinder began to turn, and Schwill threw his hand up, shoving the pistol away from his face, just as the first 147 grain, jacketed hollow point, came speeding out from the barrel.

The loud report of the first gunshot was still resounding inside the house as Schwill saw blood streaming from his left hand. His bloodied hand felt as though someone had rammed a hot poker in it and was slowly twisting it. Schwill was bellowing from the pain when he felt the cold steel of the muzzle

against his right jaw, just as Lindberg touched off another
shot.

Schwill's garbled screams cut through the smoke filled room
as the second bullet entered his head, tearing flesh from bone,
blood rushing into his mouth. Schwill thrashed about on the
floor for several seconds before his body laid still, his eyes and
mouth partially open.

Schwill laid motionless on the floor, Lindberg and another
male staring at his body, questioning each other as to whether
Schwill was alive or dead.

Inside the northeast bedroom, Robert Hester lay on the floor
holding his radio in both hands. Several males were beating him
trying to make him let go of this radio.

Hester: - (unintelligible words / screams, with sounds of a disturbance / fight in background)

One of the males pulled Hester's pistol from his holster and
walked into the kitchen. Coleman was holding Hester's heavy,
black flashlight, in his left hand, slowly tapping it into the palm
of his right.

Hester's hands were now handcuffed behind his back as he
looked up at the men that surrounded him. He saw one of the
men holding his portable radio and could hear the confusing,
non-stop transmissions coming from it.

"Why are you doing this, what did I do?" asked Hester.

Coleman answered by raising the flashlight and striking
Hester in the face, with all his might, with all the strength that
his pent up frustrations would allow. He raised the flashlight
again and struck another savage blow.

Two males who was standing in the room quickly left through the south door of the bedroom, and headed for the backdoor, as the beating continued.

Hester's nose was broken.

His skull fractured.

The blows continued.

It was only the beginning.

CHAPTER 7
Tommy Turner

Officer Tommy Turner, in car 159, slid to a stop in front of 2239 Shannon Street. Black smoke from burning brakes rolled out from underneath his car.

Turner: - **159 is on the scene.**
Dispatcher: - **159 on the scene.**

Turner could see car 128 parked against the curb on the south side of the street between 2239 and 2243, white smoke floating up from the tailpipe. He rushed from his car, night stick in hand, looking across the yards of the darkened houses for Schwill or Hester.

What the hell is going on? Turner thought.

He had expected to hear the grunts and curses of a fight, but there was nothing. He ran the thirty feet from the sidewalk to the front door which was illuminated by a porch light, glancing at the grey car in the drive-way.

Turner had been at Chelsea and Bellevue when the call for help went out. He had punched the accelerator on his cruiser, and with the four-barrel screaming, raced eastbound on Chelsea,

47

almost rolling his car as he made a sharp turn to go north on Hyde Park then east on Shannon.

Turner stopped at the front door as he looked back towards the street seeing the officers from car 129, Ricky Watson and Martin Carr hurriedly walking across the yard.

Watson: - **29 on the scene.**
Dispatcher: - **Car on the scene?**

Turner pressed himself against one side of the door watching as Watson took up a similar position on the other side. He noticed Carr was standing in the yard using one of the porch supports as cover. Turner heard no sounds coming from the house as he turned to Watson.

"Are you sure the dispatcher said 2239?" Turner asked.

"Yea, he said 2239," Watson whispered back.

Turner flung open the wrought iron security door, and kicked the wooden door twice. It sprung open with a splintering of wood. He stepped through the doorway, lights from the back part of the house casting shadows across the darkened living room.

Hearing footsteps, he looked up quickly and saw a man with a pistol run from one room to another, across a hallway. His eyes caught more movement as he turned his head to the right.

There he is, Turner thought, a shape lying on the floor near a chair, those are uniform pants. It had to be one of the officers. Turner saw that the officer was being held down on the floor by two or three men.

Watson was standing nearby, but at a different angle, and Turner would later learn, saw an officer in another room he thought to be Hester.

"Alright motherfuckers break it up!" Turner screamed.

Turner heard more footsteps, and saw another man running from the northwest room of the house. The man stopped abruptly and jumped back behind the wall. Turner looked into the room and could see the edge of a bed and a dresser. Then suddenly, a gun appeared in the doorway.

Turner dove to his left as flames boiled out of the pistol. Spinning, he came up on one knee, and pulled his pistol, bringing it up to eye level. A heavy blow smashed into the top of his head. It was followed by a second blow that struck his pistol.

He fell in a stumbling roll, backwards out the front door, feeling his radio fall from his belt. Blood streaming down his face, he struggled to regain some balance on the porch, pointing his pistol at a huddle of men near the doorway of the northeast bedroom. He pulled the trigger.

Nothing happened. The gun didn't fire. He looked down. The cylinder was open - dislodged by the blow inside. He tried to close it, but it wouldn't lock shut. The sounds of screams and running feet were all around him as he slammed his hand down on the push rod of the revolver. Live rounds tumbled to the porch at his feet.

Staggering, he ran off the porch to the northeast corner of the house looking for other officers to help. He saw no one.

Where the fuck is everybody?

Turner grabbed a breath to slow his mind then reached down, working to loosen a brick from the front porch. Then he hurled it through the northeast window. More gunshots whistled around him.

He spun, stumbling and falling as he ran for cover behind a van parked in the drive-way next door. Once behind it, he looked back towards the house as he reloaded. A bearded male, stood in the threshold of the front door, also reloading a pistol.

I'm gonna pass out thought Turner as things started getting dark and blurrier. He knew he might be blacking out, and he struggled to understand what was going on around him.

He stared at Officer Stephanie Hanscom running to his side. Hearing voices of another officer over the radio he leaned back against the van then dropped slowly to the ground.

Norton: - **42 on the scene.**
Dispatcher: - **142 on the scen...**

Reserve Officer J. Norton, Car 142, jumped from his cruiser, hearing gunfire as he sprinted across Shannon. He looked towards the house, seeing a man standing on the porch popping off rounds at officers. He pulled his radio, screaming out a warning as he ran.

Norton: - **42 shots fired!!!**
Dispatcher: - **We do have shots fired on the scene, now, shots fired, 2239 Shannon.**

Norton stopped on the sidewalk, snapping off four quick shots. The man's left arm flew up and away from his body. The man stepped back, and turned the pistol towards him, orange flames rolling from the barrel. Norton sprinted to cover, ducking behind a police cruiser parked in front of the house. Norton quick peeped over the cruiser. The man standing at the door was gone.

Officers lying behind cover listened as chaotic transmissions continued to blare from their radios.

Car 147: - **47 scene.**
Dispatcher: - **1.....**

Unknown Car - **we got........down!!! We need an ambulance!!!!**
Dispatcher: - **Ok, one down,...ne..**
Car 122: - **122 show us in and pulling over.**
Dispatcher: - **122 in and on it.**
Captain Randle: - **102....**
Unknown Car: - (unintelligible with siren in background)
Dispatcher: - **All cars signal Q. All cars signal Q, 102.**

All radios instantly fell silent on the command for quiet (*signal Q*) by the dispatcher.

Captain Randle: - **102, let us know about our officer.**
Dispatcher: - **Any officer struck on the scene.**
Carr: - **Check,..**(sounds of panting, heavy breathing) **he's hit in the head...he is not...need an ambulance for officer; officer is down, he's ok. Have... have had shots fired.**

Lt. R. B. Summers, car 104, was pushing his cruiser hard west bound on Shannon, seeing blue lights in the distant flashing off the elementary school. Summers turned off his blue lights and headlights as he locked up his overheated brakes, fish-tailing to a stop in front of 2247 Shannon only seconds after Turner reached cover. Seeing Turner and other officers hiding at the van, Summers, in a half crouch, hurriedly made his way towards his officers, wondering how many were injured.

Dispatcher: - **Ok, the officer is down. Shots were fired. The officer appears to be ok on the scene, ...ok, 102.**
Lt. Summers: - **..4 scene.**
Captain Randle: - **Ok, 102 in route.**
Dispatcher: - **Ok 102. 104 scene.**

The groggy Turner opened he eyes, and saw Lt. Summers standing over him. He tried to speak but couldn't find the energy to open his mouth, feeling himself nodding off again. He tried to push himself up to a sitting position, wishing the roaring in his head would go away.

The non-stop chatter on the radio filled the night air.

Car 127: - **127, 129 we got officers in the house still pinned down. We're gonna need some more cars.**

Dispatcher: - **Ok, officers are inside the house, 2239 Shannon, are pinned down. Do need some more units on the scene.**
Car 190: - **190, I am in route.**
Dispatcher: - **Ok, 190.**
Car 163: - **63....**
Unknown Car: - **......scene...**
Car 165: - **65 on it.**
Dispatcher: - **165.**

"Lieu..."Ray and Bobby....still in the house, think one of em... has...has... been shot." Turner mumbled.

"Cliff, get Tommy to the hospital!" Summers said.

Turner could hear Summers saying something to Woodruff, as he fell forward, hitting his face on the concrete drive-way.

As Summers watched Woodruff pull Turner to his feet, he knew he needed to check the perimeter. He moved south along the van, then crept to the corner of the house, inching his way down the east side. Seeing a window, he peered in and saw a man holding a pistol as he crawled across the kitchen floor, south towards the rear of the house.

Summers swung the butt of his gun, shattering a pane of glass and quickly fired a round. The man dropped to the floor, then tried to stand up and run. Summers sent his second bullet crashing into the man's body. The man toppled face first into a large room off the kitchen, where he lay still, his ankles and feet still exposed. Summers watched for several minutes, but the feet didn't move.

Summers knew he needed to check the back. He stepped carefully towards the rear of the house, listening to the sound of gunfire, seeing the glint of a badge on a figure near the small shed in the backyard.

Car 163: - **163.**
Dispatcher: - **63.**

He pulled his radio from his belt.
"104, tell all officers to hold their position and wait on the TACT unit," Summers ordered.

Multiple unknown Cars: - (unintelligible)

Summers cursed under his breath, realizing his transmission had been walked on by other cars trying to transmit. He inched his way north along the side of the house, then sprinted to the cover of the van. He leaned against it, catching his breath as he heard screaming coming from inside the house. But he couldn't make out what was being said. He strained his ears to catch the words as another voice interrupted.

"R.B., what the hell is going on?" Captain Joss Randle asked as he hurried up.

"We've got a mess, Joss," Summers said, as he began reloading his pistol.

"Are all our officers accounted for?" Randle asked.

"No," Summers replied, his eyes pulling back up to the front of the white house.

"Ray and Bobby are still inside."

CHAPTER 8

Russ Aiken

O fficers Russ Aiken and Cedric Canada, were at Whitney and Hollywood in Frayser when the call for help went out. Four minutes later, car 115, with Aiken white-knuckling the steering wheel, was careening east bound on Shannon. Aiken milked the spongy brakes as his cruiser, pulling hard to the left, and coming to a merciful, metal grinding stop. As the two officers bailed out of their cruiser, Aiken heard an officer imploring someone to cover the back of the house.

Unknown Car: - **Need somebody on the back of the house. Need somebody on the back of the house.**
Dispatcher: - **Need a car in the rear of the house, to seal the house.**

Officer Lisa Owens in car 141 was trying to phone in an auto theft report at Chelsea and Woodlawn when the call went out. Owen who had been on the job a little over a year, shot down Chelsea east bound before turning north on Hollywood then back west on Heard. She saw two cruisers in front of her as she rocketed to the scene.

Owens bailed out of her car with her shotgun running towards a car parked on the south side of Shannon when she heard multiple shots going off all around the house. She saw Vidulich standing by the tree and Aiken standing near a van hollering something out.

"Canada, stay with the Lieu, Watch your life!" Aiken shouted.

Aiken glanced over his shoulder, seeing that Canada made it safely to the van where Summers and other officers were standing. He moved south along the van before sprinting south down the drive-way past the three windows on the east side of the house, finally making it to a small back porch. Despite the cold, his uniform was sticking to his sweat drenched body as he crept up and across the yard to the open back door. Slowly stepping through the door, his pistol cupped in both hands, he made his way through the sunken meeting room walking the three steps up into the den.

Aiken's eyes swept the empty room, then moved past the kitchen, and to the far northeast bedroom.

Motherfucker...

He could see Robert Hester lying on the floor. Men were stomping his body, cursing at him, hitting him with his own flashlight, Hester's body jerking with each blow.

Ripping his radio from his belt, he shouted into it.

Aiken: - (unintelligible screaming)**...they're getting beat! they're getting...**(unintelligible)
Dispatcher: - **Ok, the officers inside the house are still hollering for...**

Two muzzle flashes split the darkness - silent flashes of light that Aiken couldn't hear and he didn't know why, but he keyed his mike again, shouting into it a second time.

(Unintelligible, male officer screaming)

Dispatcher: - **The officers are still calling for assistance inside the house.**

Then suddenly more gunshots, Aiken could see that someone in the bedroom was firing at him. He returned fire, his hands and ears strangely numb to the recoil and explosions. He spun to his left, the room alive with more muzzle flashes coming from two more men standing at a doorway on the western end of the den.

Lt. Summers: - **...4 there is shots in the house we are gonna have to go in.**
Dispatcher: - **Ok**

I'm fucked, Aiken thought as he stumbled backwards, frantic for some cover. He turned and dove across stools, then head-first over the home made bar. A few seconds later, he peered up over the bar. He saw more muzzle flashes streaking from the northeast bedroom. A man, with a light colored shirt, lay motionless on the floor in the kitchen.

Aiken rolled out from the bar, and down the steps into the sunken meeting room, and crawled out the back door. He stumbled to cover near the fence at the southeast corner of the house. Leaning against it, his heart racing, he opened the cylinder and dumped the five empty hulls, and unknown to him at the time, one live round to the ground. He reloaded his last six rounds, then without hesitation, crept up and back through the rear door, slipping again into the sunken meeting room. Gunfire erupted immediately, lighting the room with an orange hue as each shot flashed in the darkness from near the bar.

**Vidulich: - 121, we got to go inside, there still being fired...inside.
Dispatcher: - Ok, 121 is advising there are still shots being fired
inside the house.**

Aiken shot his pistol dry before turning and diving headlong
out the back door. He was tumbling into the yard as a fusillade
of bullets splintered the back door behind him. Glass was shattering everywhere.

He crawled to the corner of the house, his chest burning as
cold air rushed into his lungs, but his mind was working fast - trying to figure out what else he could do. He scanned the yard,
and saw an officer standing ramrod straight, holding a shotgun.
He climbed to his feet, grabbing the fence to keep from falling.

"Bring me the Goddamn shotgun," Aiken rasped as he reached
out and grabbed the Remington, 12 gauge, pump-shotgun from
the dumbfounded officer. Aiken opened the action half way, making sure a round was in the chamber as he stalked back to the door.

A window exploded with a deluge of bullets over his head,
showering him with glass. He turned and fired a load of 00 buck
through the same window, working the action, then firing a second load at a man inside.

Aiken was working the action to fire a third time when he
heard a male voice screaming out the window.

"I'm gonna kill this mother-fucking pig if you fucking pigs
don't quit your fucking shooting."

His body running on pure adrenalin, and hot with frustration, he froze for just a second, knowing he could not go back
inside. Not after hearing that.

He retreated from the window, handing the shotgun back to
the officer, who Aiken saw, had not moved from his rooted spot
by the fence. He leaned against the side of the house, sucking in
more cold air, trying to figure out what to do.

"Stay here and watch the back!" Aiken yelled at the officer.

No matter what he did, he needed more ammo. He also had to tell the Lieutenant what happened. Aiken ran north along the drive-way to the van. The radio was still crackling with traffic when he saw Summers and Randle at the van. Aiken hurried to them, his words rushed and fast.

"Lieu the son-of-a-bitches shot an officer twice while I was in the house," he said.

"Help secure the rear of the house, stand-by until the TACT unit relieves you," Summers said.

"Lieu, I shot up all my ammo, you got any extra?" Aiken asked.

Summers reached into his pockets, filling up Aiken's outstretched hands with bullets. Aiken reloaded his pistol, also filling up his six round belt loop, dropping the extra bullets in his pants pocket. He looked back at the house, his chest still tight, his mind still racing.

He thought about the order he had been given. Hold the perimeter, wait on TACT. He thought about disobeying it, thought about going back inside. He ran a hand through his hair. Shards of glass and wood splinters fell like a winter shower from his hair and into the palm of his hand. He stared at them.

Then his gaze moved to the front yard. Officers scampered about, blue lights cast an eerie purplish hue to the air, and radios cracked with a steady stream of directives and counter-directives.

Then screams, coming from inside the house, Aiken dropped his head, his heart gripping with anger.

Please don't let that be an officer.

Help,...help me!
P-L-E-A-S-E...!

59

CHAPTER 9
Ed Vidulich

C ar 121, Officers Edward "Big Ed" Vidulich and William "Winky" Downen were inside Conway Tobacco Company on Front Street, near the Mississippi River, talking with employees when they heard Schwill's voice come over the radio.

Car 128: **- 128, start us another car over here.**

Something in his voice made Vidulich and Downen stop talking in mid sentence as they listened more closely to the radio.

"Winky, something's going on, did you hear Ray?" Vidulich asked.

"Naw,...they're okay." Downen replied, with little conviction in his voice.

"I'm telling you Winky something's wrong," Vidulich said.

"Yea, let's get back to the car," Downen answered.

Vidulich climbed behind the wheel as Downen sat in the passenger seat, quickly leaning over to turn the volume up on the car mounted radio.

Vidulich guided the cruiser north on Front as transmissions of officers acknowledging Schwill's request for another car came across the radio.

Dispatcher: - **Ok 128, 129, at 2239 Shannon, back up 128, possible wanted party, 2239 Shannon.**
Car 129: - **29.**
Car 159: - **59 disregard my special, show me in route to meet em.**

Dispatcher: - **Ok, 159.**
Car 147: - **147, do you want me to pull down that way?**
Dispatcher: - **Ok, 147.**

"Ed, you gonna get up on Chelsea in case it breaks bad?" Downen asked.

"Yea, I'm thinking we get on Chelsea and head that way until we hear it's okay," Vidulich answered.

"Do you know where were going?" Downen asked.

"Naw, look it up," Vidulich replied.

Downen began flipping through the map book as Vidulich headed east on Chelsea crossing over Thomas.

Schwill: - **128, HELP !!!**
Dispatcher: - **128 is calling for assistance! 128 is calling for assistance! 2239 Shannon, Ok, 147.**

"Shit!" Vidulich and Downen yelled in unison.

The cruiser hesitated slightly then jumped forward as Vidulich stomped his foot on the accelerator while flipping on the blue lights and siren as Downen called out directions from the map book.

Downen grabbed the radio mike, cursing under his breath as he tried and failed to transmit to the dispatcher that car 121 was on the way.

Unknown Car: - (unintelligible)
Dispatcher: - **Couldn't read that number.**
Unknown Car:- (unintelligible, with siren in background)
Unknown Car: - (unintelligible)
Dispatcher: - **Cars pulling down I can't read your numbers.**
Car 142: - **142.**
Dispatcher: - **142.**
Downen: - **21.**
Dispatcher: - **121.**

Vidulich was milking the steering wheel through a blurry rush of houses, trees and store fronts, the scream of the siren and pumping blood pounding through his ears. Then Downen's voice finally reached him.

"Ed, left on Hyde Park, ED, left, left, goddamn it!" Downen screamed.

Vidulich turned the wheel hard left feeling the cruiser begin to slide, then vibrate violently as it shot up Hyde Park.

"Okay Ed, about the fourth street up turn back to the right on Shannon!" Downen yelled over the wail of the siren.

Vidulich realizing he was about to miss Shannon mashed the brake pedal, hopping the curb as he turned back east on Shannon. In the distance, he could see half-dozen cruisers parked haphazardly in the street. He slid to a stop in front of the drive-way of 2239 Shannon.

Vidulich held down the release button, slapped open the locking arm and pulled the shotgun free, then ran to the large oak in front of the house. He saw that Downen had rolled out and was running around to the rear of the cruiser.

Vidulich glanced around the scene. Officers were running in what seemed like total confusion. He could see Aiken rushing to the east side of the house, then disappearing from view as an officer's excited voice asked for someone to cover the rear of the house.

Unknown Car: - **need somebody on the back of the house, need somebody on the back of the house.**

Over to his left, he saw Hanscom behind a cruiser parked in the street, pointing her shotgun at the house. Her normally placid expression was replaced with one of disbelief. Vidulich glanced back to the cruiser.

"Winky, you still at the car?" Vidulich hollered.

"Yea, I'm watching the west side, Downen replied.

Downen was down on one knee, looking south along the narrow drive-way as he counted three windows on the west side of the house, which was no more than twenty feet from the duplex next door.

"Get back inside!" Downen hollered, waving his hand at a woman standing on the parking pad in front of the bricked duplex at 2235/2237 Shannon.

Downen glanced to his left seeing Cliff Woodruff guiding Turner, his face covered in blood, to a cruiser, then watching as the it sped off. His eyes shifted back to the house.

"Ed, can you see anything?" Downen yelled.

"Motherfuckers keep running by the door!" Vidulich yelled, as he kept his eyes on the front sight of his shotgun. The barrel was aimed at the open front door, and he strained to see past the glare of the porch light, into the darkness of the house.

Radios crackled continuously and the night air filled with shouts, gunshots, and sirens. Vidulich couldn't believe it. He thought he had seen it all in his five years on the job, but he had seen nothing like this.

Then he heard more shots, coming from inside the house, followed by an officer's voice screaming over the radio.

Aiken: - (unintelligible screaming**.....their getting beat, their getting**....unintelligible)
Dispatcher: - **Ok, the officers inside the house are still hollering fo.....**
Aiken: - (unintelligible, male officer screaming)

Vidulich keyed the mike on his radio as the voice faded away.

Vidulich: - **121, we got to go inside, there are still being fired... inside.**
Dispatcher: - **Ok 121 is advising there are still shots being fired inside the house.**

Vidulich wedged the shotgun hard against his right shoulder, frustration rising inside him as he pointed it at the front door, looking for a target. But he realized that he couldn't risk a shot with officers still inside. His ears caught the pop-pop of more pistol shots sounding from somewhere at the rear of the house. He ducked as a shotgun discharged off to his left and he let out a muttered, "damn."

He wheeled around in time to see smoke rolling out of the shotgun in Hanscom's hands.

"Stephanie, don't shoot! Bobby and Ray are still in the house!" Vidulich screamed.

Vidulich stared a moment longer at Hanscom as she lowered the shotgun from her shoulder, then turned back towards the house. Several more pistol shots were answered by the loud reports of a shotgun from a firefight he couldn't see being waged somewhere at the rear of the house.

The voice of his partner caught his attention.

CHAPTER 10
Ray Schwill

I t hung suspended above the floor, its beauty a sharp contrast to the ugliness all around. It was delicate, each small piece joined with others, to form a larger whole. Prisms of glass that held light briefly, then gave it back in reflection.

It was one of so many reflections that night, from the yellow-white flash of guns, to the blue hue of the lights through the windows, to the red stain of spattered blood. And the unmoving body of an officer sprawled in the living room floor.

Schwill opened his eyes a sliver, seeing the chandelier but nothing else. He could feel blood running down his face, dripping into a pool on the floor. He could hear gunfire and hoarse cries and shouts coming from inside and outside the house. The static voices of a nearby portable radio floated to his ears, the sound muffled by feet stomping across the carpeted floor. Gunshots, lots of gunshots, more than he could count, were echoing through the house and into his throbbing head.

He knew he was still alive, but he was afraid to move, fearing someone was still watching him. Knowing he had to get out of the house, his eyes shifted, catching the top corner of the wooden door.

Only have to get one door open.

He guessed he was probably ten feet away, and wondered if he would be able to stand up and get to it. His big six foot frame could cover the distance in three long strides, but he knew he had lost a lot of blood, and his whole body pulsated with pain.

His left hand felt useless and stiff. His jaw was numb and felt funny on right side, burning like hell. Knuckles and fingers on his right hand were stiff, knee wrenched, throat aching so badly he couldn't swallow. No way could he fight his way out. He knew that.

He could sense someone in the room but he fought the urge to move any part of his body other than his eyes. His mind held no illusions has to what these crazy motherfuckers were up to. They wanted to kill some cops. But he didn't want to die curled up in this shit hole.

He knew he would have one chance to get out the door, if it didn't work, his wife would be without a husband and his two kids without a father.

David Jordan stood in the darkness of the house no longer wanting to stay, but afraid to leave. Sweat, dirt and blood stained his shirt and face. There was so much shooting going on, he was afraid to look out a window with all the bullets flying. Everywhere he turned he could see the flashing of blue lights flooding in through the curtains. The sounds of sirens told him there had to be hundreds of cops out there.

This was truly the hell that Lindberg had described in their discussions. The darkness, the resounding noise and so much blood.

Jordan thought he was going to die. JuJu had been shot already. Jordan could hear him in the den moaning and crying. He knew JuJu was only eighteen, just a kid, still living with his mama. Knew, too, Lindberg had been shot. Knew his arm was bleeding. Knew he was in the house now, but not sure where.

Jordan squatted against the wall of the kitchen listening to the gunshots, wishing he was home right now with his wife Jackie and his five kids. He wished he had run out the back door with T.C., Ray and the others. He knew it was too late now.

If he ran out now, he knew Lindberg would shoot him in the back or the cops would shoot him to pieces, either way he knew he was fucked.

Jordan stood up and started through the kitchen, towards the west door as screams of anguish from the northeast bedroom reached his ears. He glanced to his right into the living room, at the cop's body lying on the floor. He peeked around the corner through the glassed security door. That big white cop was still standing by the tree with his shotgun. Jordan took a deep breath, then sprinted across the hall through the east door of the northwest bedroom.

Schwill felt the eyes of a man standing in the kitchen, then saw a blur of movement as the man ran past the hallway door. What in the hell is going on wondered Schwill.

He could hear voices in the room. Someone else was watching him from near the fireplace, but Schwill couldn't see him clearly, barely able to discern a silhouette, with a bushy afro, his body rocking from side to side. The familiar sound of .38 caliber revolvers, firing off in volleys, exploding through his ears as the sound of running feet faded from the room. In the chaos, Schwill knew his chance to escape was close. He would have to be patient, wait for the right time.

Jordan walked through the northwest bedroom, wanting to keep an eye on the windows like Lindberg had told him to do. Make sure no one - no pigs - got in. He checked the single curtained window over the bed, never stopping his movement as he walked out the south door, directly into the southwest bedroom.

He saw the window was ok, the curtain still in place. He was turning to go out the door when bullets shattered the window, the blast exploding through his ears. He dropped to the floor and started to crawl.

Then a burst of more shots, coming from outside the northeast bedroom. When he thought he was clear, Jordan jumped up, running through the meeting room, tripping over a slithering Andrew Houston. Jordan pulled himself up, and ran to the northeast bedroom.

There was one man left in the room to watch him. Schwill knew if the man would just turn his head, or just leave for a moment, he could get out of here. There would not be a better time than now. Come on asshole, Schwill thought; turn your head away one more time.

The distant report of a shotgun blast, along with the shattering of glass and curses came from the northeast bedroom, but Schwill tried to keep his eyes fixed on the man standing by the fireplace. He had turned towards the sounds of gunfire.

He could hear screaming now at the rear of the house, intermingled with the roar of gunshots being fired inside, both in the northwest bedroom and from the back of the house.

The man turned and ran to the northeast bedroom, squatting down on his knees as he stopped in the door. Schwill could see the soles of the man's shoes.

Schwill rolled on to his side, wincing with pain as he unsteadily climbed to his feet, the fresh, salty taste of blood in his mouth as it spilled down his throat.

He staggered toward the door, shapes in the background, sparking with intermittent flashes of gunfire from the darkness in the back of the house. Schwill hit the door with his shoulder as he fell against it, banging at the latch with his hand. Cold air slapped him in the face as the door swung out.

You can do it...

"Ed, somebody's coming to the front door!" Downen yelled.

"Shit, that's Ray, Winky!" Vidulich answered.

Schwill stumbled off the porch into a blinding kaleidoscope of blue lights, his every step growing weaker. He raised his hands to steady himself, but there was nothing to grab.

"I'm gonna get him, Ed!" Downen screamed. He left the cover of the cruiser, running for the figure stumbling out the front door.

"I gotcha, Ray, I gotcha!" Downen said.

Then an arm around his waist words being shouted into his ears, but Schwill couldn't understand anything being said couldn't see anything except blue uniforms. But he knew they were police officers. He stumbled towards the wall of police cars parked in the street. He could see officers waving at him to hurry.

Approximately 9:16pm

Vidulich: - **121, we gonna need a ambulance this location we have an officer shot twice.**

Dispatcher: - **Check, an ambulance is in route.**

Downen could feel the warmth of blood on his arm as he wrapped it around Schwill's waist guiding him towards the street.

"It's okay Ray, it's gonna be okay," Downen repeated as he helped Schwill move to cover.

Vidulich watched Downen and Schwill run to a cruiser parked on Shannon before slowly turning his gaze back to the front door. It was splashed with blood.

Schwill started to feel himself fall as he reached the cover of a cruiser. He tried to stay up as he fell against the car and on to the street. He looked up at the officer screaming at him to get up, get to cover.

I just can't do it, thought Schwill, as he laid his head down on the pavement and passed out.

CHAPTER 11
Tim Helldorfer

Timothy Helldorfer, New York born and a graduate of the University of Mississippi, was a four year veteran of the department. He rode the West Precinct, affectionately known by officers within the department, as the "wild west" and home to a group of "Charlie" shift officers who dubbed themselves "The Coneheads". It was the smallest precinct but included most of the housing projects, the hospital district and downtown.

When the call for help went out, over the West Precinct radio, Helldorfer was with Dan Chalk riding in 432.

West Dispatcher: - **We have an officer calling for assistance at 2239 Shannon. This will be north of Chelsea one or two streets going back north of Chelsea.**

The two West Precinct officers were at Central and East Parkway, about eight minutes away. Helldorfer, who was driving, asked Chalk if he knew how to get to 2239 Shannon.

"Hit Hollywood and go north till we pass Chelsea," Chalk said.

Helldorfer pushed the accelerator to the floor heading east bound on Central. He looked to his right at the darkened outlines of the Mid-South Coliseum and the Liberty Bowl Stadium before spinning the wheel hard left going north on Hollywood.

With the needle pegging eighty-five and climbing, Helldorfer roared by the Board of Education Building, taking his foot off the accelerator as he saw the red light at Hollywood and Union. He milked the brakes watching for traffic on Union.

"Are we clear right Dan?" Helldorfer asked.

"Check right, Tim," Chalk answered back.

West Dispatcher: - **Okay, 425 is on the scene advising we have officers on the inside and shots are being fired, 2239 Shannon. All cars in route to that location be advised shots are being fired at that location.**

Officer Randy Oliver riding in car 476 had been at Poplar and East Parkway when the call went out, four minutes later he was pushing his cruiser hard up Hyde Park before turning east on Shannon.

Sliding to a stop west of 2239 Shannon Oliver jumped from his car running towards cruisers parked closer to the house. He saw Schwill lying on his side bleeding from his face and left arm.

"Ray, did you get hit?" Oliver asked.

"Yea," Schwill whispered.

"Where at?" Oliver asked.

"My head and hand," Schwill answered.

"Ray, do you want to go to the hospital or stay here?" Oliver asked.

"I need to go to the hospital, where's your car?" Schwill asked.

Oliver pointed to his cruiser as he and Schwill made their way through the maze of cruisers parked on the street to Oliver's car.

Helldorfer felt the little Dodge jump as he stomped the gas. He stared at the roadway ahead as four minutes ticked by. He didn't hear Chalk calling his name the first time.

"Tim,..Tim! We're coming up on Chelsea," Chalk repeated.

"Okay which way?"

"Go back west on Chelsea and cut north on Hyde Park," Chalk said.

West Dispatcher: - **All cars in route be advised there are two male blacks inside the house armed. Still have an officer inside the house...Okay all cars be advised shots are being fired at this time inside the house, we have one officer down inside the house and they do have his radio, 2115hrs.**

Helldorfer turned the wheel hard left, feeling the cruiser slide as he went through the intersection, then spun it back right careening north up Hyde Park, as the cruiser with Oliver and Schwill, with its blue lights and siren on, sped past him south bound on Hyde Park. Helldorfer then turned back right on Shannon seeing blue lights flashing atop silhouetted cruisers parked all over the street. He slammed the cruiser into park, west of the house.

Oliver turned west on to Chelsea from Hyde Park glancing at Schwill who had laid back in his seat. Oliver cut down southbound Watkins headed for Methodist Central Hospital as he was finally able to get on the air to advise the dispatcher what he was doing.

West Dispatcher: - **All cars be advised of location and set up road blocks. I think they are coming in the squad car.**

Oliver: - **Check, 476, Southbound Watkins at Parkway we are two minutes from Methodist Central.**

West Dispatcher: - **Okay, southbound on Watkins from Parkway at this time in route to Methodist Central.**

Helldorfer and Chalk heard Oliver on the radio as they ran to a black and white parked sideways on the northwest corner of the yard near the driveway and the great oak tree.

Both took cover behind the cruiser. The officers assigned to this car, car 435, Renfro and Mhoon, were crouched behind the car, their weapons trained on the house. It had been Renfro and Mhoon who had taken the original purse snatch report.

Helldorfer listened to the pop-pop of gunfire coming from all around the yard, occasionally seeing the muzzle flash from an officer's gun. He saw Vidulich, his friend from Ole Miss and fellow New Yorker hiding by the big oak, shivering with cold. Helldorfer thought of the winters in New York as he shuddered, moving his feet trying to stay warm when he heard a strained voice talking on the North radio.

Officer Hester: - **28x I'm inside the house,.. being held hostage, stay away from the house they're holding me hostage. I repeat,.. stay away from the house.**

Helldorfer watched several officers key up their mikes wanting to answer Bobby.

Unknown Cars: (Several mikes key up with no voice. Background noise from communications personnel can be heard.)
Officer Hester: - **128x,... 128x, stay away from the house, they're holding me.**
Dispatcher: - **128x is advising they are holding him hostage. He's advising to stay away from the house.**

Helldorfer cocked his head, listening as the highest rank-ing supervisor on the scene, Captain Randle began issuing a directive to the officers on the scene that was repeated over all frequencies.

Captain Randle: - **102, 102.**
Dispatcher: - **102.**
Captain Randle:- **102, I believe we have an officer being held hostage inside the house. All those men who are not in a cov-ered position, back, let's get those cars moved back off Shannon Street. Start on the west end, west portion of Shannon, let's move all the cars back, on the east end, let's get in cars. Let's move them back.**
Dispatcher: - **Per 102, move all the cars back on both the east and west end of Shannon.**

One officer is being held hostage.

Helldorfer looked at the slew of cruisers parked all along Shannon packed in bumper to bumper with blue lights flashing, coloring the city block with a purplish hue.

He ran back to his cruiser, got inside and turned off the blue lights. He saw the little street called Hazel running northbound from Shannon just west of the house as he gunned the engine. He pulled the car to the end of the street near the northwest cor-ner of the school, running back to the scene as Downen passed him in a cruiser. Helldorfer ran to another cruiser parked in front of the house slowly backing it up, catching a glimpse of Downen and other officers running towards abandoned cruisers.

Helldorfer ran back down Hazel, his lungs on fire, finally slowing to a walk while moving to the next cruiser. When he was done, he stopped, squatting down behind a cruiser, his back to the house, trying to catch his breath. A car door slammed nearby. He continued to squat for several seconds as he watched his cover being driven away by Downen. Helldorfer, the former Greek games obstacle course champ, quickly sprinted to the next car.

He pulled the next cruiser behind the school parking lot, near the cafeteria, then walked south back along Hazel. He looked west down Shannon, seeing his former Captain from the West Precinct walking towards him.

"Hey, Chief Moore!" Helldorfer called out.

"Tim, what's the situation?" Chief Inspector Jackie Moore asked.

"Chief, Ray got shot inside the house but he made it out right before I got here.

Bobby Hester is still inside and it sounds like they beating him," Helldorfer said as he told Moore what little he knew.

"We've got to go get him!" Moore, the former TACT commander, barked with his face tightened in a grimace.

Moore knew what needed to be done as he stared at the house seemingly oblivious to the bedlam surrounding him. He knew the situation needed to be stabilized and a plan of action devised before entry was made.

First things, first, need to recon the house, Moore thought. "Tim, I need to look over the perimeter. Grab a shotgun and come with me!" Moore ordered.

Helldorfer ran to his cruiser, pulling the shotgun free from the gun rack. He chambered a round from the magazine into the chamber while trotting back to where Moore stood.

"Ready Chief," Helldorder said.

"Alright Tim, let's start on the west side and work our way around towards the back," Moore answered.

Helldorfer walked slowly south along the drive-way on the west side of the fence, the shotgun tucked tight against his shoulder, his eyes shifting from the house back to Moore. He stopped moving as he felt the light tap of Moore's hand on his back, waiting quietly until he felt another single tap on his back, before continuing to walk along the south side of the house.

Helldorder could feel beads of sweat on his forehead as thoughts of a Chief Inspector he was entrusted to protect getting killed ran through his mind. He led Moore around the back of the house and up the east side feeling himself breathing easier again. Moore tapped him while pointing towards the houses east of 2239. He walked along side Moore east across the front yards to the intersection of Shannon and Boxwood. As the two men walked, radio transmissions alerted Moore to the location of the temporary command post.

Unknown TACT Car: - **Advise 502 he can come north on Boxwood to Heard. The lane is clear up that way.**
Dispatcher: - **502, you can go north on Boxwood. The lane is clear that way.**
TACT Lt. Jim Pugh: - **502.**

Helldorfer saw TACT Officers standing in the intersection dressing out in their tact gear. Lt. Pugh spoke with Captain Jim Music. The TACT van, with its doors opened, was parked on the east side of the corner house.

"Officer you can leave now," Music said.

"Captain, I was ordered by Chief Moore to stay with him," Helldorfer answered.

"It's okay Tim, head back to your post," Moore told Helldorfer.

As Helldorfer walked back west to his previous position the radio crackled with more radio transmissions.

Car 1001: - **1001** (Director Holt) **to 1000** (Mayor Hackett).
Dispatcher: - **10....**

Lindberg Sanders (on police radio): - **Hey, you listening? Hey, you listening out there? .... HEY!!!**

Unknown Car: - **We're listening, go ahead.**
Unknown Voice: - **Hey, you,... Goddam it. Hey, I,...I was over here all day,... yea.**

The last voice was new. It didn't sound like a police officer. It didn't sound like Hester, either. It sounded like a black man. A pissed off one. And Helldorfer paused for a moment on the frosted grass, realizing it was one of the men inside the house, using Hester's radio.

What a nightmare this was, he thought. It was a situation no one could have imagined. Somebody taking a police officer hostage while close to a hundred police officers had their weapons trained on the house from outside, somebody inside was now taunting the officers with a police radio.

He looked down toward the house.

Every available officer stood shivering in the darkness, hoping that an opportunity might come to save Hester. Neighbors were being evacuated from their homes. Sirens still wailed. Lights still turned. And behind him, TACT officers were putting on ballistic vests and loading M-16's.

And now the Director of Police Services was involved.

And the Mayor.

As the angry, raspy voice on the radio faded off, Helldorfer started walking again.

Man, could things get any worse?

CHAPTER 12

Steve Parker

Officer Stephen Parker, car 163, was in the 2800 block of Overton Crossing on a complaint call with another one man car when the shots fired call went out.

Car 142: - **42 shots fired!!**
Dispatcher: - **We do have shots fired on the scene now, shots fired, 2239 Shannon.**

Parker told the other officer to finish up the report as he jumped into his cruiser and headed southbound on Overton Crossing. He turned left and shot down east bound James to McLean. Two minutes later he was roaring down Chelsea. As he neared Hyde Park his blue lights went out and as he looked down at the light bar panel box he over shot Hyde Park. He jammed on the brakes and as two other police cruisers roared by on Chelsea he made a U-turn and followed them up Hyde Park to Shannon. As he made the right on to Shannon he could see the cruisers and blue lights in the distance his radio alive with frantic voices.

Unknown Cars: - (unintelligible....**9**.....)
                (.......**start the TACT unit**)
             (unintelligible)
Dispatcher: - **The TACT unit is being started.**
Unknown Car: - **need a location on Shannon.**

Dispatcher: - **Runs north off Hyde Park, north of Chelsea.**
Unknown Car: - (unintelligible with siren in background)
Car 542: - **542 on the North end.**
Unknown Car: - **15..... we do have a male black inside.**
Dispatcher: - **Ok, we do have a male black inside.**
Car 542: - **Ok, 542..... give us a location again.**

Parker stopped his cruiser in the middle of Shannon just east of Hyde Park and sprinted east along the street. He saw Vidulich posted up at a large tree in the front yard as he ran into the yard of the red bricked duplex. He had heard something about a duplex on the radio as he ran to the fence surrounding the duplex at 2235/2237 Shannon. As he scaled the fence west of the duplex his radio blared with desperate voices.

Watson: - **129, there are four or five people in the house along with the two officers. They've got the officers pinned down inside the house......**
Unknown Car: - **That's on Shannon.**
Dispatcher: - **Check th......**
Vidulich / unknown car: - **21..**(unintelligible).
Dispatcher: - **21 go ahead, other car stand by.**
Vidulich: - **121 we need an ambulance.**

Approximate Time 9:18pm
Dispatcher: - **Ambulance in route.**
Watson: - **Car 129 were gonna need two ambulances.**

Dispatcher: - **Ok, on two ambulances.**

Parker keyed up the mike on his portable radio trying to find out which duplex he needed to watch.

Unknown Car: - (unintelligible, sounds of radio being keyed up several times.)

Cursing to himself he tried once again to raise the dispatcher.

Parker: - **Is it the east or west duplex?**
Multiple Cars: - (unintelligible)**.....do we have any officers in the rear of the house?**
Parker: - **Which side of the duplex is it, I can cover the rear.**

Parker crouched by the fence in the rear of the duplex and could see Aiken at the corner of the white house next door.

Aiken stopped at the southeast corner of the house peeking around the corner at the glass strewn back yard. He edged his way along the south wall feeling the cold brick of the house through his sweat soaked uniform shirt as he stepped towards the rear door.

Parker keyed up his mike again trying to verify which side of the duplex he needed to watch.

Parker: - **163 is it the west or east duplex?**
Dispatcher: - **Is it the west or east duplex?**
Unknown Car: - **It is not a duplex, it's a house, a white house.**
Dispatcher:- **White house, not a duplex.**

Parker looked over the fence at the white house. He could see that a door on the southwest side of the house was standing open as was the door on the south side that Aiken was crouching by.

Aiken inched his way across the yard glass shards breaking under his shoes sounding to him like cannon fire in the silent darkness as he bent down peeking in the window. He glanced up and saw Parker standing in the yard next door.

"Parker, come here." Aiken said, as he waved at Parker.

Parker climbed the fence and slowly moved to the west side of the door peeking around the door frame into the house.

Both could hear transmissions from a police radio coming from somewhere in the house as Aiken moved closer to the window when bullets fired from inside showered him with glass the echoing sounds of the shots rolling across the yard.

Parker retreated back to the duplex to cover the open west side door as Aiken moved to the southeast corner of the house.

I hope we're doing the right thing Aiken thought as jumbled radio transmissions interrupted his thoughts.

Captain Randle: - **102 we have a officer who has been shot, Officer Schwill is on the way to the hospital.**
Dispatcher: - **102, the squad car has taken one officer to the hospital.**
Unknown Car: - **Is there an officer in the rear of the house?**
Dispatcher: - **Is there any officer in the rear of the house, now?**
Car 3132: - **3132, 3133 has the rear covered.**
Dispatcher: - **3132, 3133 has the rear.**
Multiple Unknown Cars: - (unintelligible) **.... at the rear of the house with the flashlight turn it off, your silhouetting everybody.**

Captain Randle: - 102, 102 to all cars. Start on the house on the east side, correction on the west side, get those people notified make sure that they're down if we can lets evacuate them.

Parker moved to the rear door of the duplex and knocked on the door. After several seconds the door to 2237 Shannon cracked open and Parker told the people inside that they needed to follow him. Parker moved to 2235 and again knocked on the door telling the people inside to follow him. He led the occupants around the south side of the duplex and on to Shannon Street before running back to 2237. He went into the back door found a chair and sat down at a window that faced the southwest side of 2239 Shannon his shotgun resting across his legs. Parker would remain at his post for over three hours listening to the voices over the radio.

Approximately 9:21pm
Hester: - 28x I'm inside the house,.. being held hostage, stay away from the house they're holding me hostage. I repeat, stay away from the house.
Unknown Cars: (Several mikes key up with no voice. Background noise from communications personnel can be heard.)
Hester: - 128x,... 128x, stay away from the house, their holding me.
Dispatcher: - 128x is advising they are holding him hostage. He's advising to stay away from the house.
Car 545: - 45 to 502 we have two of the cars here, TACT unit cars, at Boxwood and Heard. We're dressing out.
Dispatcher: - Ok, 502.

Car 502: - 502 advise them to stand by there.
Car 102: - 102, 102.
Dispatcher: - 102.

Hearing Hester's voice on the radio was both a relief and a curse to Aiken as he leaned against the southeast side of the house, letting out a long sigh. He figured Hester might already be dead.

"Well, if he's talking then he's breathing." Aiken thought.

He knew he would have to do something he hated.

"Damn it to hell." Aiken thought.

He could feel the anger surging through his body thinking that no officer who was worth a damn wanted to sit back and wait. He thought of his academy training that had conditioned him to act and react immediately.

If something is wrong, get to it now, Aiken seethed.

He listened as 542 and 502 spoke on the radio. He knew what that meant. The TACT unit was here. They would get Hester out of there. Aiken was confident in the knowledge that anything a patrol officer couldn't handle the TACT boys could.

"P-L-E-A-S-E..."

CHAPTER 13

Dispatcher Jim Wiechert

North Precinct Radio Frequency - 9:22pm

Lindberg: - **I know this is some bullshit you know it is bullshit, your ass is going to burn tonight. And you know it, You know it. Come on. I want you to get WLOK. Call WLOK the radio station do you understand.**
Unknown Car: - **Okay, we will get WLOK, now keep it cool inside. We will get the radio station keep it cool, yeah.**
Dispatcher Jim Wiechert: - **WLOK will be contacted, everything is under control.**

L indberg stood in the northeast bedroom, his head turning as he looked out the north window, then the east window. Every where he looked, pigs running, hiding by the house, parked all over the street with their fucking blue lights flashing.

He held his left wrist against his chest, blood oozing from the gunshot wound in his forearm and staining his brown shirt. In his right hand, he clutched the cop's portable radio. The pain shooting up his left arm and through his fingers only increased his anger at the devils surrounding his house. They will all burn for this, Lindberg thought. He brought the radio to his mouth and spoke into it, his voice hoarse with anger.

Wiechert: - **North is being used as a primary, standby on this frequency. All cars on the scene go to car to car frequency. Go to car to car frequency all cars on the scene.**
Lindberg: - **I want you to know I can see all through this bullshit.**
Unknown Car: - **Yeah.**
Lindberg: - **Yeah, try it, let those mother fuckers try it. Turn the other radio back on and turn it on quick, NOW!**

Wiechert slammed his hand down with frustration causing the other dispatchers in the room to jump. What in the hell is he talking about Wiechert thought, as he took another drag off his cigarette.

Lindberg paced about the living room and northeast bedroom, looking from the blue-hued windows to the strange reflections on the walls and then down at Hester's huddled form on the floor of the bedroom. The radio jerked back and forth against his lips.

Wiechert: - **We have the radio on, we are listening to you, go ahead.**
Lindberg: - **I am not the one you want.**
Wiechert: - **Go ahead we are listening to you.**
Lindberg: - **That is not the radio I am talking about man.**
Wiechert: - **We have everything under control go ahead and talk to me.**
Lindberg: - **Did you all do what I told you?**
Wiechert: - **Check, we contacted WLOK right now.**

Lindberg: - **Get me WLOK before I blow this motherfucker's head off.**

WLOK was a Memphis radio station. Why Lindberg was asking for them, no one knew. At this moment, all Lindberg had was a police radio and one other human voice to talk to - the North precinct dispatcher, Jim Weichert.

On the 12th floor of the Criminal Justice Center at 201 Poplar, Wiechert stubbed out another cigarette in the ashtray. He held his empty coffee mug aloft briefly before sitting it back down near his ashtray. He was a notorious chain smoker who only took a burning cigarette out of his mouth long enough take a drink of coffee.

He had sat down on the North radio at 8:00pm and had waved off other dispatchers who had volunteered to relieve him since Hester and Schwill's call for help had went out.

The communications office was 70 feet long and 30 feet wide, with windows that over looked the river and the rest of downtown. Against the east wall were rows of cubicles where dispatchers sat answering calls for police assistance. The five radio consoles, for the four precincts and the traffic bureau, were situated along the west wall of the room, with the supervisor's office on the north side of the room.

The dispatchers working other radios had switched their secondary channel to north and listened in while dispatching on their primary.

Greg Hudgins had been working the west frequency when Schwill had called for help.

Hudgins had immediately broadcast the information to the West Precinct.

91

Hudgins: - **We have an officer calling for assistance at 2239 Shannon. This will be north of Chelsea one or two streets going back north of Chelsea.**

As the next hour wore on, Hudgins sat at his console feeling helpless as he listened to Lindberg rant and rave. Hudgins had moved west cars from the southern wards of the precinct up to the North Precinct to answer other calls not related to Shannon Street.

The South dispatcher had moved his cars north to cover the vacated west wards. The East dispatcher was sending cars to cover the Raleigh and Jackson area wards of the North Precinct.

The communications office or radio room as it was known by those within the department was in total chaos. Every phone seemed to be ringing with off duty officers and command staff, who couldn't get through to their own precinct, calling communications to find out what was going on.

The "Charlie" shift supervisor on duty was responsible for making phone notification with all bureau heads. On a typical high level event, this would have involved calling one or two Captains or maybe a Deputy Chief. On this night he and the senior dispatcher had called the heads of every bureau, the entire command staff, the Director and the Mayor.

Through all the bedlam, Wiechert sat hunched over his console smoking cigarettes, drinking coffee and talking with Lindberg Sanders.

Wiechert: - **We have got WLOK contacted and they are on their way.**
Lindberg: - **Get that radio on quick!**
Wiechert: - **We have got it, we have got the radios on, go ahead I am taking to you, talk to me. Go ahead and talk to me, what**

else do you need besides WLOK, we have got WLOK on the way.

Lindberg: - (inaudible.)

Wiechert: - **Will you say that again, I didn't understand you.**

Lindberg: - **I want C.J. Morgan!**

Wiechert: - **C.J. Morgan from WLOK, is that right?**

Lindberg: - **Get them away!**

Lindberg: - **Do you hear?**

"Get away from the window motherfuckers!" Lindberg screamed at the silhouettes he saw near the east window.

Wiechert: - **Yeah we know that we are getting them away as fast as we can.**

Lindberg: - **Get them away from the window!**

Wiechert: - **Yeah we are moving them away now.**

Lindberg: - **Do you hear?**

Wiechert: - **Well if you can't see anything they must be moved all back out of the way now.**

Lindberg: - **Motherfucker, don't you tell me.**

Wiechert: - **I'm not, I am just relaying the information to you.**

Lindberg: - **I didn't tell you to call WEEE radio, you motherfuckers better not start any shit, its messed up bad, tell them out there asshole.**

Wiechert: - **Now if you want somebody from WEEE radio.**

Lindberg: - **I know damn well you could get to them quick couldn't you?**

Wiechert: - **No, we are not calling them, the only one we are calling is WLOK.**

Lindberg: - **You do what somebody else tells you, now you going to do what I tell you now.**

Wiechert: - We just called WLOK, is there anyone else you want down there? Is there any other members of your family, or your preacher you would like?

Lindberg: - Talk with no mother fucking dogs, I am tired of telling you what to do, mister. You better get somebody tell me somebody that is able to tell me something, let me start talking to them, do you understand?

Wiechert: - Okay give me you phone number and we will get...

Lindberg: - You don't get a fucking thing, just start if you can't get the paper down there, we are getting rid of this mother fucker, shit is going to start.

Wiechert: - Okay it would be easier to let us talk to you on the phone from WLOK.

Lindberg: - Don't talk to me like I was a dog, I am standing here with,.. in other words I am standing here with the dude, not you... Do you hear?

Wiechert: - We are not telling you to. We said if you want to talk to WLOK...

Lindberg: - (inaudible)

Wiechert: - Okay it is going to take a long time for us to get a radio to WLOK we all need..

Lindberg: - That would take too long then, now uh

Lindberg: - Did you understand? Say it again.

Hester: - Help...help

Wiechert: - Yeah, I heard that. Heard that fine.

Lindberg: - What did he say?

Wiechert: - He said I understand partner.

Lindberg: - Then what..

Wiechert: - I don't know you turned the radio off. I could not hear him.

Lindberg: - Goddam liar, what did he tell you to do?

Wiechert: - **You turned the radio off I could not hear him. Put the radio up there and let him tell me again.**

Lindberg: - **Here then..**

Hester: - **Help, help. Somebody help.**

Wiechert: - **Son of a** (inaudible).

Lindberg: - **You can do it two ways, that is the wrong way man, I know** (inaudible) **and you don't understand. Black preacher** (inaudible) **did you understand that?**

Wiechert: - **Yeah, I understood that.**

Lindberg: - **Are you still working at it?**

Wiechert: - **Yeah we are working on it. Let me get Mr. Morgan to talk to you.**

Lindberg: - **You still got them around the house have you?**

Wiechert: - **I don't know, we are trying to move them out now, it takes time.**

Lindberg: - inaudible

Wiechert: - **We are trying to move them out.**

Lindberg: - **You a goddamn lie.**

Wiechert: - **We are trying to get them out of the way.**

Lindberg: - **They got a shotgun at the window, better move the fuckers away do you hear?**

Lindberg: - **Did you hear him?**

Wiechert: - **No, I didn't hear him, can you get him to say it again.**

Lindberg: - **Wait a minute he is going to talk to you.**

Wiechert: - **Okay I am here.... Can you put the officer on the radio for me?**

Lindberg: - **You just wait, you don't tell me anything motherfucker.**

Wiechert: - **No, I am not trying to tell you anything, we just want to make sure the officer is still alright.**

Lindberg: - **Get them off my back house.**

Wiechert: - **I am up here on the radio talking to you on the radio, I don't know about your backyard. I want to know if that officer is alright?**

Lindberg: - **You mother fucker, do you want to hear his head blowed off, mother fucker...**

"Help..no,..please stop.."

"P-L-E-A-S-E..."

CHAPTER 14

TACT

They were coming, men whose eyes were devoid of emotion. They had heard the call and were even now racing to the scene.

At approximately 9:20pm TACT officers T. L. Todd and W. D. Dawkins arrived in the equipment van at Boxwood and Shannon and began setting up telephone communications. Lt. Pugh, car 502, arrived shortly after and conferred with Captain Randle about the present situation.

All four precinct dispatchers had put out the same call on their frequencies.

All 500 cars switch north, all 500 cars switch north.

Everyone knew the 500 cars were TACT officers.

Pugh immediately began sending TACT officers to cover the inner perimeter. Melton, armed with a .223 rifle, was sent to the roof of the school to cover the front of the house. While other positions for containment were being sought out.

When TACT made the scene their first priority was to confine or contain the threat to as small of an area as possible. This containment would not be complete until all four sides of the house were covered with TACT officers. This first area of containment was considered the inner perimeter.

TACT car: - **at 2238 the first street from the house, advise 502 that the house is vacant, can put a sniper on the roof, fire shots in the back of the house.**

Melton (car 540): - **I am elevated on the school building across the street, if you could get one back here that would be good, both of us would be at the same level. Advise 502 there is some movement on the left window, right window is clear, have a metal vent door going in the front.**

Pugh sent York and his .223 bolt and scope rifle to the vacant house at 2238 Curry to cover the rear of the house.

Melton: - **Movement in the window.**
Pugh: - **502 to 540**(Melton) **and 542**(York)**, operating on the yellow at this time, we are operating on the yellow at this time.**
Melton: - **540**
York: - **Okay 542.**
Dispatcher (F-5): - **Okay 542, show you okay operating on the yellow.**
York: - **542, code yellow check.**

Off duty TACT members K. McNair, D. Rutherford and Sgt. Huff arrived on the scene.

Pugh told Huff to evacuate civilians in the immediate area, locate a command post for the TACT unit, and to form an assault team for an immediate entry if the need arose. Pugh looked over at the school knowing they needed a large area to accommodate the negotiators and their command post, which had to be separate from the TACT command post. The school could also house the command staff, family members of any suspects inside the house, the press and the perfect place for officers to rest when they were rotated off outside posts.

Pugh: - **502, will you contact school security and have them meet us at Boxwood and Heard?**

Sgt. Huff stood with the assembled TACT officers in the intersection of Boxwood and Heard. He appointed McNair the team leader. Todd, Dawkins, D. Rutherford and H. Ray would be the entry team. The entry team would be the men who would force entry into the house, should it come to that.

TACT officers Summers, Cockrell and Gallo armed with M-16 assault rifles and 12 gauge pump shotguns, worked their way over to 2237 Shannon to cover and contain the west side of the target house. TACT members Godwin, Watson and Jones, also armed with shotguns and M-16's, were assigned to 2243 Shannon to contain the east side of the house. The assault team followed behind and would use this house as the jumping off point for any entry on the house. Sgt. Huff secured 2247 Shannon as the Command Post for the TACT unit command staff.

One of the TACT officers who took up a sniper position in the vacant Curry house was Ronnie McWilliams. He had been home when the fight and shooting had occurred. McWilliams, who had been in the TACT unit since 1980 knew he had to get to the scene.

He had left his house and driven to the West Precinct on Avery off Hollywood and picked up the TACT van assigned to him. After making the scene, he had dressed out and been briefed at the TACT command post inside 2247 Shannon. He made his way to the Curry address, after the briefing. When he took up his position alongside York, he had his 30-06 bolt and scope, and his .223 bolt action rifle with a night scope.

Other TACT officers were at positions in and around the yard of 2239 Shannon. Their first responsibility was to prevent any attempt at a "push out," or attempted escape, by any of the suspects. The temperature was in the low 20's with a bone chilling wind as the TACT officers watched from their positions of containment.

Exposure to the extreme cold necessitated the rotation of the officers on the inner most perimeter. The rotation process was slow and exceedingly dangerous.

Pugh: 502 to 540, are you in need of a relief? 502 to 540, 502 to 542.
York: - **Check 542.**
Pugh: - 502 to 504, send an officer we can use as a spotter relief, send one officer.

The TACT officers could not allow their positions to be discovered or lost. Ground taken was ground to be held onto as every foot was precious. Each man knew that an assault on the house could be ordered at any time. TACT officers also provided intelligence information to the command staff.

It was an accepted fact that the TACT Unit was comprised of the best trained men in the department. They were men who knew their job like few others. And on that night, they laid out in the open, staring at a small white house, and shifted the weight of their M-16s or sniper rifles knowing that, if just given the chance, they could free Bobby Hester.

Everyone out here knew Hester was being beaten. Everyone out here knew he would die if the order did not come soon enough. But the order was not coming and they were left with their one painful question.

Why won't they let us go in?

They already had a plan. They knew it would work. It had worked at St. Jude hospital less than twelve months ago.

In July of 1978 six year old Robert Michael Goulet had been diagnosed with leukemia and was brought to St. Jude Children's

Research Hospital in Memphis. The hospital had been founded by actor Danny Thomas. It was named in honor of the saint of the hopeless.

After two years of treatment at the facility the little boy died on December 27th, 1980.

On, Thursday, February 4th, 1982 the young boy's still distraught father walked into St. Jude. French-Canadian Jean Claude Goulet, armed with a .357 magnum revolver, took four hospital employees hostage. Goulet wanted to make the world aware that the cause of leukemia needed to be found. He believed that finding a cure was not as important as was learning the causes.

Approximately thirty-four hours later, the TACT unit was told by negotiators, that Goulet had begun writing a suicide letter. Captain Meeks, a member of the negotiation team, said that members had attempted to calm Goulet down. The assault would have been called off if Goulet could have been calmed down. Because of the fear that Goulet was preparing to execute hostages, the TACT unit began the implementation of their plan.

Three TACT officers, J. Birdsong, J. Filsinger and D. Hubbard moved to the door from the outside hall. Following close behind the three officers was TACT officer J. Thurman, who was armed with an M-16.

Hubbard hit the door with his body, knocking it open. Birdsong and Filsinger dived on top of hostages. Thurman fired four rounds at Goulet. All four rounds struck Goulet in the chest and head killing him instantly.

The TACT unit knew what their job was and they knew what the procedure was. When talking failed to resolve the situation then it was their job to move in. They were there to save lives. It was a cold hard fact that sometimes in order to save a life; they must take the life of another. It wasn't pretty or poetic but it was their job.

Inside the TACT Unit, life was measured in importance by who you were. The lives of hostages and police officers ranked ahead of the criminal, the hostage taker. The TACT unit was conceived out of necessity.

TACT officers were not mindless men with a death wish or cold blooded assassins. They were professionals. They trained non-stop for hours on end for entries that would last no longer than a few seconds. Their mission was no different than that of the negotiators. They just did it in a far more dangerous arena.

The same TACT officers who now surrounded the little white house on Shannon Street thought back to ST. Jude. It hadn't been that long since they had stood in the halls of the hospital. This whole situation here on Shannon was without reason. How could everything go right at St. Jude and everything here seem so wrong?

That wasn't a civilian screaming inside that house. It was a policeman *and* a hostage; the top priority on their unchanging list of who was the first to be saved in a hostage crisis.

They had gone into St. Jude's to save staff members who Goulet had not yet harmed. And now, they were forced to lay in the cold and listen to a police officer beg for the same merciful action.

Melton (roof of school): - **540 to 502 the subject is clear of the building, will you search and screen, sounds like somebody calling for help again.**

"Please stop hurting me..."
"Somebody, make them stop..."

Car 162: - **More screams coming now.**
Dispatcher: - **Advise more screams out.**

It would work here. Just give us the order.

Unknown car: - **We have got somebody in the right window, on that room yelling, moaning and carrying on.**

Seconds ticked by, but no order came.

Melton: - **Appears screams are coming from the right window.**

"Help me,..please God..."

Car 165: - **Advise someone is screaming and hollering no.**

"No, No, help me.... Please."

Melton: - **540 these screams are,...they sound like a male, white, evidently it sounds real clear, they may have a window open on front.**

"Oh, God...mama"

And the tears began to fall.

"P-L-E-A-S-E..."

CHAPTER 15

Negotiators

It was 9:50pm when hostage negotiator officer Jeff Larkin pulled up to Hollywood and Heard. He had been at home when Captain Lewis, Hotel One, had called him. Larkin had been one of the primary negotiators at St. Jude. Larkin was with several uniformed officers as they stood by their cruisers parked in the street on west bound Heard. Larkin, like the officers standing with him, just stared at the empty street and listened to Lindberg on the radio.

Lindberg: - **Just a minute, are they shooting in the back?**
Wiechert: - **No sir, we don't want anyone to get shot down there.**
Lindberg: - **Sure don't, you been shooting in here that motherfucker, loud mouth, ain't nobody done no bullshit, god damn, you listen a little while ain't nobody going to listen to no bull shit, you better get your shit right now, get them fellas off from around here. Preacher,...I am asking you to preach now.**

Eight minutes later Lt. Parker and Officer Mark Pfaffenroth pulled up and parked their cars. The three negotiators were driven to Shannon and Boxwood. The officers listened to Wiechert and Lindberg talking over the radio as they stood by at the TACT van which had been designated as the temporary command post for the negotiators. Other negotiators found their way to the command post and waited for their boss to brief them as the sounds of Lindberg's voice echoed through the group.

Lindberg: - **Just a lie mother fucker, you're a mother fucker.**
Wiechert: - **I didn't hear that last one.**
Lindberg: - **Talk to me do you, you won't do it my way do you?**

Captain Lewis walked up to the assembled group and began the briefing.

"We have an officer who has been taken hostage inside a house at 2239 Shannon. We do not know how many suspects we have but one is talking over the North primary channel to the dispatcher and has been doing so for approximately forty-five minutes. We do not know the condition of the officer. All cars have switched to north car to car. Crews, you're the primary on this one. Dunlap, you're the coach. Pfaffenroth and Torrance will be the recorders. Larkin, Stepter and Shotwell will be back-ups.

The main office at Shannon Elementary School will be our primary negotiation post. A female called the radio room earlier and advised the man who owns the house is named Lin."

The group had listened intently; there was none of the usual banter on the scene, not with a police officer involved. The negotiators walked north across Shannon into the school playground before turning west and entering the school through the northeast doors which had been opened earlier by school security officers.

The main office was situated on the southwest side of the school directly across the street from 2239 Shannon and directly below the sniper positions on top of the school.

Crews, who had borrowed Captain Music's portable radio, got on the air at 10:24pm.

Crews: - **My name is Crews, I am a police negotiator can you talk to me on the radio for a minute?**
Lindberg: - **Sure can.**
Crews: - **How is the officer doing in there?**
Lindberg: - inaudible.
Crews: - **I didn't hear you, you cut yourself out, come back again please.**
Lindberg: - **I want to talk to WLOK, that is who I want to talk to now.**
Crews: - **We are trying to get in touch with them; it is late at night, got to give us a few minutes, okay?**
Lindberg: - inaudible
Crews: - **I can't hear you Lin.**
Lindberg: - **You can hear me now,** inaudible.
Crews: - **Okay Lin, Okay Lin.**
Lindberg: - inaudible...**mother fucker.. they shooting and growling.**
Crews: - **We don't want any shooting now.**

Lindberg walked through the living room before turning left down the hallway then right through the northwest bedroom, glancing at JuJu as he lay against the east wall moaning. As he walked he spoke into the radio.

Lindberg: - inaudible

Crews: - **I didn't hear what you said Lin, can you speak a little slower?**

Lindberg: - inaudible.
Crews: - **Lin, how about letting that officer come outside?**

"These mother fuckers don't know who they're dealing with."
Lindberg screamed out as he walked through the den.
"Get away from the house mother fuckers, do you hear me?
Get your fucking asses away!" Lindberg hollered.

Unknown Car: - **He is in the rear of the house, can hear him yelling at the rear of the house at this time.**
Unknown Car: - **Demanding everyone get back.**

"These devils will all burn!" Lindberg shouted as he stood in
the middle of the den. Lindberg grinned as his followers let out
defiant screams of burn devil.

York (Curry house): - **542, I am close enough to hear them in the rear of the house, he has got the people in the house excited, this house backs up to the back door, let's keep our people away from the house.**
Unknown Car: - **He has gone back to the front of the house.**

Lindberg walked through the kitchen, stopping as he entered
the northeast bedroom. As he looked down at Hester he keyed
the mike.

Lindberg: - **I am going to blow this mother fucker's brains out if you don't get your shit together.**
Crews: - **What do you want us to do, Lin?**
Lindberg: - **You are still trying to play tricks.**
Crews: - **We aren't trying to play tricks, I just come on the radio and I don't know what you want.**

Lindberg: - **To talk to Mr. Morgan...inaudible...listen to the radio and you are talking to tell,.. tell them to talk to somebody else too.**
Crews: - **Okay Lin, I am talking to you on the police radio, not the plug in radio or the table radio. Okay? Did you hear what I said Lin?**
Lindberg: - **Y'all are fucked up real bad ain't cha? You not going to do like it is supposed to be done.**
Crews: - inaudible.
Lindberg: - **Like nothing. Cause you.. inaudible.. You are going to fuck up and get blowed away. Now get your goddamn ass back ain't you? ..inaudible..Just fucked up ain't'cha?..inaudible.. You ain't going to fuck up this time are you?**
Crews: - **What?**

While Crews labored in his negotiations Captain Music was having his own problems. Music had earlier requested that the utility company make the scene to have street lights cut off along Curry, which was the first street south of Shannon. Pugh and Music were inside 2247 Shannon when they saw a M.L.G.&W. truck drive by the C.P. west bound on Shannon. As they watched, the truck slowed down, almost stopping in front of 2239 Shannon, before it continued on westbound then northbound on Hazel.

Command Post: - **Can we get that Light, Gas and Water truck stopped on the scene?**
Command Post: - **C.P. to any personnel, stop that Light, Gas and Water, we do not want him going in front of the house.**
Randle: - **102, Light, Gas and Water truck came by, I have got him stopped here, what do you need?**
Unknown Car: - **Check with 500.**
Unknown Car: - **Okay, how about turning the lights off on the street over on Curry, don't let him go back in front of that house.**

Command Post: - C.P. to 104, R.B., we need to get him over there on Curry and let him cut off the lights over there on Curry. Just don't let him come back this way.

Negotiators huddled inside the school office listened as Crews tried to develop some kind of rapport with Lindberg. As they listened to him rant, the members wondered if he would calm down enough to be reasoned with. Once family members arrived and were interviewed, negotiators would have some insight into Lindberg and the causes for his pent up anger at police.

At a few minutes after 11:00pm negotiators were advised that WLOK disc jockey Morgan had been located.

Dispatcher: - Check 106 if you are at the command post, tell the negotiators that demand for Mr. Morgan, we have located him and he is being brought to the command post.

At approximately 11:30pm Director Holt held a staff meeting along with Harold Ray, Deputy Chief of Investigative Services; Tom Marshall, Deputy Chief of Uniform Operations; Sidney Cole, Chief Inspector of General Investigations; Fred Warner, Chief Inspector for Special Investigations; A.L. Williams, Chief Inspector Special Operations and S.O. Jackson, Inspector for Security.

Holt told those gathered that Lindberg was holding a cocked pistol to Hester's head; in addition it was believed that the hostage takers were high on either alcohol or drugs.

The consensus of the command staff was not to assault the house due to the likelihood that Hester and officers of the entry team would be seriously injured or killed.

While the staff meeting convened, negotiators prepared to interview Morgan; they traded ideas amongst themselves as Lindberg continued to talk.

Crews: - **We want to talk to you on the telephone; will you give me your telephone number?**

Lin, give me your telephone number so I can talk to you on the phone so we can keep this conversation thriving.
Lindberg: - inaudible.
Lindberg: - **Nasty, mother fuckers, dog face**,.. inaudible.
Hester: - **Help!..aaaah.. Help!**
Parker: - **I am hearing calls for help, I can't tell if it is coming from inside the house or not.**
Dispatcher: - **Okay, 163 advises he is hearing calls for help, not sure if they are coming from inside or not.**
Melton (school roof): - **Check 540,...they are coming from inside.**

"Help me,..STOP..."

"P-L-E-A-S-E.."

CHAPTER 16
Fun Bunch

Relatives and friends of those suspected of being in the house on Shannon Street found their way to Shannon Elementary School. By bus, by car, they came, through the crowds of onlookers, past the police lines, and into the school building.

Family members and friends who had arrived at police lines were escorted into the school and placed in a classroom on the northeastern side of the school.

Waiting for answers to their questions they found instead, questions they had to answer. The questions and answers ran together over time. They all wondered what was going on in the little white house and silently prayed for the safety of their loved one.

Alfredea Mckinney, who was Lindberg's sister, told investigators about his mental illness. She related that when Lindberg began to read the bible he had told her not to eat pork or drink water. Sanders had told her that the world was going to end of January 11th, 1983.

Annie Thomas had made contact with police and told them she thought her husband Earl Thomas was in the house. She told investigators that Lindberg had two sons that he frequently beat. She said that he and his followers often smoked marijuana.

She had not seen him since Friday, January 7th.

Negotiator Parker: - **Who is in there with you, is Earl Thomas in there with you?...Answer me Lin is Earl in there with you? Is everybody else in the house okay, we know your are not in there by yourself, we want to know if everyone is okay, is there anything we can do for any of them?**

Lindberg: - **Don't worry bout me I'm doing your mother fucker, don't worry about him.**

Parker: - **What about you Lin do you need anything, Lin? We know your are in charge in there, that's your place and you are in charge but you have got to take care of those people in there and there is other people out here asking about them. Tell me if Ronald is in there with you?**

Lindberg: - **Don't matter who is in here with me.**

Parker: - **Ronald in there with you Lin?**

Lindberg: - ..inaudible.. **you know what, don't matter blow your fucking head off, God damn.**

In Annie Thomas' opinion the men most likely in the house were David Jordan, Bo Jack, Cornell Walls, Reginald McCray, Pete and Fred, who were brothers.

Dorothy Thomas Sanders, Lindberg's wife, came to Shannon Elementary.

Car 763: - **I have the wife here at Shannon and Hyde Park.**

Dispatcher: - **Command post, command post...command post, command post. 763 the command post was at Boxwood and Heard and obviously has moved to Shannon Elementary, if you can see your way clear from Boxwood and Heard carry her to the command post at Shannon Elementary.**

She told investigators and negotiators of her difficulties with her husband and his religion.

In 1973 Lindberg began receiving in-patient treatment for a delusional mental illness. He was re-admitted in 1975 and never worked again after his release in that same year. Sometime after his release, he had, for almost a month, hid beneath his house. His family could not find him and thought him missing.

He continued out-patient care all through the seventies and early eighties. His last visit had been on December 22nd, 1982. She had moved out of the house on Shannon in early January of 1983. The constant fighting, over religion and of Lindberg not taking his medication, had forced her to live elsewhere.

"How long has he been off his medication?" an investigator asked.

"About three weeks." Dorothy said.

He told her that one day, the moon would come down to the earth and all those who had failed to follow his words, would be burned to death.

She went to the Shannon house on January 8th to take Lindberg some fish and wine. He had told her she needed to leave because only men were allowed. Her last conversation with her husband would come at around 5:30pm on January 11th. He spoke with her on the phone. He asked if she would pick his jogging suit up from the cleaners and asked her when she was coming home.

She called the Shelby County Probate Court offices, on Monday, January the 10th, begging to have her husband committed immediately. She was told the process would take several days. She told the clerk that was not good enough. When the clerk suggested that Dorothy call the police, she replied that the police couldn't do anything, unless, he was trying to hurt himself or someone else.

She had hung up the phone in frustration. She knew Lindberg needed help but the system had failed her. She told investigators and negotiators she never knew just how deep her husband had fallen. She said she believed that Pete Murphy, Squeaky, Michael, Scrubb, Earl and her son Larnell were probably in the house.

She told officers that there was an old man that used to live on Alston that Lindberg called, Jesus Christ. She thought that he might be able to talk Lindberg into giving himself up.

She volunteered to take investigators with her to help find the old man.

Lucinda Sanders, Lindberg's thirty year old daughter, had accompanied her mother to the school. She told investigators that her and her mother had gone to the house on January 8th, at around 1:00pm, to see her father. Lindberg had asked Dorothy to prepare fish for him and all the disciples. At one point during their visit Dorothy had interrupted Lindberg while he was reading his Bible and he had jumped up and knocked her down, screaming at her to leave the house and never interrupt him when he was reading the Bible.

She said her father and his followers did not drink water or eat pork, but that smoking marijuana was part of the teachings of the Bible.

She related how Lindberg had given her his favorite Bible and told her of his prophecy.

"Lucinda, the world is coming to an end in three days." Lindberg said.

"You and Dorothy will have to leave, only the disciples can be here in the house when end comes." Lindberg said.

Lucinda said she had seen about fifteen men in the house.

"Pete Murphy, Squeaky, Larnell Sanders who is my brother, Michael, Scrub and Earl are the only ones I knew by name." Lucinda said.

12:40am
Car 165: - 165, advise someone is screaming and hollering no.

Thomas Macklin, Lindberg's brother, came to the school at somewhere around 1:00am on January 12th, and told investigators he would help try to talk Lindberg into to letting the officer go.

When Macklin entered the office he saw two cars parked in front of the 2239 Shannon.

"That Maroon, Buick there belongs to T.C. and that other one is Squeaky's." Macklin said, as he pointed to the two cars parked in front of 2239 Shannon.

Negotiators asked officers on the roof to try and obtain the tags on the two cars parked across the street and a yellow, Continental parked in front of the window of the office, in the circular drive of the school.

Officers were unable to see the tags on the two cars parked in front of the house but did obtain the tag on the yellow car, 1SL799. The tag was checked and showed registered to a David Jordan of 1090 Ayers.

2:00am
Holt held a staff meeting in the cafeteria of the school with Ray, Marshall, Cole, Moore, Warner, Williams, Jackson and Music. The staff was updated as to what had transpired since the first meeting. The new intelligence data showed both defensive and aggressive behaviors by Lindberg and the other suspects.

Moore told those gathered that he and members of the TACT unit had moved close to the house where they heard what sounded like hammering, which they took to mean those inside were barricading the house. He also heard Hester screaming and the sounds of a physical beating.

Jackson provided background information on Lindberg which indicated he and his sons were avid hunters. An informant, who knew the Sanders family, said there were numerous rifles and shotguns in the house.

The staff again decided to continue negotiations.

Approximately 2:45am, January 12th, 1983

Crews: - **Lin how about picking up the radio and talking to me for a minute. Thomas wants to say something to you. What did you say? Push the mike button in and talk to me Lin.**

"Bring Thomas back up here." Crews said after he unkeyed the mike.

Crews: - **Thomas wants to talk to you now, how about hanging the phone up and letting him call you on the phone? Hang the phone up now Lin, Thomas wants to talk to you on the phone.**

"Tommy, do you remember how to work the radio?" Crews asked.

"Yes sir." Macklin replied.

"There is the button you push, call him again and tell him to hang up the phone you want to try him on the phone." Crews said.

Macklin: - **Hey, this is brother, Lindberg hang the phone up.**

Crews dialed the phone number and handed the phone to Macklin.

(Phone ringing)

"Hello." male voice answering phone.

"Who is speaking?" Macklin asked.

"Who do you want to talk to?" male voice.

"Lindberg." Macklin said.

"You got the wrong number." male voice.

"Who is speaking?" Macklin asked.

"Mac." male voice.

"Who?" Macklin asked.

"This is the Macme residence, Lindberg don't stay here." male voice.

"Okay, thank you." Macklin said as he hung up the phone.

"What did he say?" Crews asked.

"Said Linberg don't stay here." Macklin said.

"Okay, maybe we dialed the wrong number."

Crews dialed the number again and got a busy signal.

Macklin: - **Lindberg, this is your brother speaking, really what do you want, they really don't want to hurt yall, if you can would you talk to me Lindberg.**

"That's okay." Crews said.

Macklin: - **Please do you mind speaking to me on the phone, that way no body get hurt so we can negotiate with you. Do you mind coming to the phone?**

"Hold the button in till the red light comes on Tommy, then talk." Crews said.

Macklin: - **Please do you mind putting the phone on the hook, please, we are trying their best to negotiate, they don't want any-body hurt Lin. They don't want the officer hurt and they don't nobody hurt inside the house and we really don't want you to get**

hurt Lin. Do you mind putting the phone on the hook so we can call you? Lin, please do that for me. Lin this is your brother, they want to come to some kind of arrangement they also don't want nobody to get hurt, so they can help you.

The number was dialed again, the line was still busy.

Macklin: - **Lin, this is your brother, who do you want to talk to? I know you want to talk to me, hang the phone back up.**

"Who do you think would be the next best person to talk to Lin?" Crews asked.

"My mother might, he might listen to her." Macklin said.

"What about Dorothy?" Crews asked.

"He might answer the phone." Macklin said.

"Now we don't want him to talk to anyone that would get him excited. Would your mother excite him?" Crews asked.

"Well,..you know how upset she is." Macklin replied.

"What about your sister, she is his daughter right?" Crews asked.

"Yeah, if we get somebody on the phone but once he gets on the phone need to.." Macklin began answering.

"Have Morgan on the phone?" Crews asked.

"Need to get Morgan on the phone right away." Macklin said.

"But we have had Morgan up all night." Crews said.

"If you could get him back over here, if any way possible, we don't want to see that officer hurt and we don't want to see him hurt. You know?" Macklin answered back.

While negotiators tried to make contact with Lindberg officers surrounding the house suffered in the unrelenting cold as they continued to watch and listen.

Car 565: - **565, show me in position on the roof of the school. The spider man up here needs relief he has been up here a long time, get somebody up here.**
Dispatcher: - **Okay 565 you okay in making the relief?**
Car 565: - **I am in position on the roof, relieving Melton and the spotter up here needs to be relieved.**

Some who sat out in the bitter weather strained to answer the voice that cried out to them...

Car 569: - **569 to 511 the house is open all the way through from the rear, if there were...**
Car 511: - **511 to 569 this is a negative on the last idea.**
Dispatcher: - **569, did you read 511?**
Car 569: - **Check.**

The wait brought out bitterness and sarcasm...

TACT Lt. Maxey: - **503 to 500 we need to see if we can safely get someone up to the house where the perpetrator is, the negotiator here have not heard from the perpetrator in some time on the radio, what they want to do is to get your man in position and notify us to see if he can hear the officer's radio.**
565 (school roof)- **565, be advised that the last scream of the officer was approximately ten or fifteen minutes ago.**
Maxey: - **OKAY, 563,.. are you close enough to the house to hear a RADIO.**
563 (school roof)- **Negative, we are over here across the street.**
unknown (school roof) - **there is movement in the house, apparently they are making preparations for a long night standing.**

TACT Lt. Pugh: - **502 to 565 we need to see if any broadcasts such as information you have been putting out may hinder us, whatever our plans are.**

unknown(school roof): - **OKAY.**

> *"No, please stop.."*
> *"Help me.."*
> *"P-L-E-A-S-E..."*

CHAPTER 17

Hospital

As relatives of the hostage takers congregated in the school, a similar gathering was taking place several miles away, at Methodist Hospital Central, 1265 Union. Friends, relatives and co-workers of Schwill and Hester stood or sat together in small groups.

When Bobby was rescued or released, he would be brought here to be treated for any injuries. His wife Anita had come to the hospital to await her husband's arrival. Family and co-workers kept a close vigil over her and shielded her from the media in a first floor room.

Turner had been transported to Methodist North Hospital in north Memphis. He was being treated for a possible concussion and was being stitched up in the Emergency room. He would leave within a few hours.

Car 3130: - **I am transporting officer to residence now.**
Dispatcher: - **Officer's name, 3130?**
Car 3130: - **Officer Turner.**

No one really considered the possibility that Bobby would not make it out of the house alive. Officers at the hospital tried to stay updated as to the situation on Shannon. Any elation felt, when told that Bobby was still alive, was tempered by the fact negotiations were at a standstill.

Officers, at the hospital, kept any misgivings they felt to themselves. Doubt began to creep into their minds as to how the situation was being handled by the police administration. The doubt would only increase and begin to gnaw away, at the wall of self confidence, each officer had erected.

Stories relayed to the officer's, at the hospital, about Hester begging for help, were not repeated in front of Anita and other civilians.

Off duty officers were coming to the hospital from Shannon Street. Their conversations, with fellow officers, were being held outside the hospital, where no one could see their anger or hear their curses of frustration.

It had been 10pm when the phone rang at 3793 Station Way off Winchester and Mendenhall. Officer Wayne Hightower answered the phone and received chilling news from Officer Dennis Wilson.

"Wayne, this is Dennis, Ray's been shot in the head and Bobby's been taken hostage." Wilson said.

"What?..tell me what the hell happened. Hightower asked.

Hightower had rode in 128's ward for five years and had been partnered with Schwill before going to the midnight shift at the North Precinct just ten days earlier. Hightower instantly recognized the address and the name Lindberg Sanders as Wilson relayed what had happened.

Hightower had made numerous calls to 2239 Shannon, arresting both of Lindberg's sons on several occasions for narcotics violations. He had always remembered Lindberg as being relatively quiet.

He had gotten dressed and took off to Methodist Central. Thirty minutes later he had stood by his old partner's bed.

"Wayne, how's Bobby?" Schwill asked.

"He's okay, Ray." Hightower said as Schwill's wife choked up and began to cry.

Hightower only stayed for a few minutes before leaving the room to talk to officers in the waiting area. It was here he learned that Hester was laying inside the house being beaten and crying for help. After a few hours at the hospital he had driven back home his mind racked with thoughts of Ray and Bobby. Another thought had run through his mind as he steered his car along the deserted streets.

That could have been me.

Helldorfer came to the hospital to see Schwill. He had walked in and put his hand on Schwill's chest. Schwill had immediately told him to get his cold hand off his chest as both shared a quiet laugh. Helldorfer looked at the left hand that was heavily bandaged up to the wrist and the gauze laying over the right jaw line, near the ear. He was surprised how alert Schwill was. Helldorfer left the room after a short visit and drove home in silence, mulling over what he had witnessed. Before he had left the scene he had heard that Director Holt and several officers had been in an argument over when an attempt to rescue Bobby would take place.

"Director, you've got to get Bobby out of there, now!" several officers had allegedly said.

"You officers should have taken care of this and I wouldn't have to make the decision." Holt had supposedly replied.

The number of officers, both on duty and off, at Shannon Street, was now well over one hundred. Some would later estimate that over two hundred officers were present.

Car 100(North Precinct Inspector): - **100 to 104.**
Summers: - **104.**
Car 100: - **Have all of your people cleared? We understand at this point that we want to have to replace those people with the oncoming shift, so any people that you have assigned at any place at this point, advise the 4-12 shift that they can be relieved.**
Summers: - **Check, all officers that have been relieved are being advised to return to precinct except the ones with the units who haven't had anybody to come down and relieve them yet.**

Parker was still sitting in the duplex covering the south west side of the house as the North Precinct Inspector tried to get the North Charlie shift officers relieved.

Car 100: - **Okay 100, that will be Cunningham, Parker and I think we have one or two other people, those people won't get relief from the 12 to 8 shift. The TACT unit will take up the slack left by them at this point.**

Summers: - **Alright, 104 to 163 and 105 if you copy, see if you can get out of the area so you can relieved.**
Parker: - **163 TACT unit advised they have got the rear of the house covered.**
Summers: - **Have you got any TACT unit officer with you?**
Parker: - **Negative 163, I am by myself.**
Summers: - **104 to 500, Captain have you got someone to relieve Parker, he is at the duplex on the west side of the house in**

question, do you need someone over there with him. He advised he does not have a TACT unit officer with him and he is covering that side.

Music: - **He has got his instructions, R.B., we don't need anybody there with him.**

Summers: - **Did you copy 163?**

Parker: - **Do you want me to stand by for a while?**

Music: - **Pull out!**

Unknown car: - **...Negative, stay there.**

Dispatcher: - **500, was the decision of 163 to stay in his position?**

Music: - **Check command post, stay in position.**

The media, hounded the mayor and top police officials, with questions concerning the number of officers present and the lack of control over the officers.

Each officer carried the same thought in their mind. That could be me in there. I could have been the one. It could be my family at the hospital waiting for me.

Ray Maples, president of the police union, complained that the department was unorganized in their handling of the situation. He like so many officers felt entry should have already been made.

If Hester was a civilian the TACT unit would have already made entry. That was the thought and complaint of officers, who were openly voicing their displeasure, to anyone who would listen. Why must we always have to put up with more shit than the rest of the world? Why are we expendable? Why don't we go get Bobby out of there?

Back at the school, Vidulich, was scrounging about in the cafeteria, looking for something to eat. He was among other things hunger and thirsty. He had stayed at the tree for over an hour. It was the coldest he had ever been in his life. He had finally pulled back under the watchful eye of the TACT unit.

Car 540: - We observed a man coming away from the tree are going to try and move him back to the command post.

After giving a statement to the Security Squad/Shoot Team, who were part of the Internal Affairs Bureau, he had went straight to the cafeteria.

Opening a refrigerated cabinet he located the treasure for which he searched. Rows and rows of half pint containers of milk stood in neat rows.

He grabbed hold of several cartons, as a lone silhouette, approached in the semi-darkened kitchen. Recognizing the man immediately, he tossed a carton of milk to the late comer, while the two chatted briefly. Vidulich walked from the kitchen, with his meaty hands holding cartons of milk, like they were fine china. As his footsteps grew faint, the second scrounger leaned against the wall. Mayor Hackett, finished off his milk, in silence.

Officer Pfaffenroth, hurriedly walked to the TACT command post, located inside 2247 Shannon. After he stepped inside, he had begun conferring with several members of the TACT unit. As two of the heavily laden officers, walked to the center of the living room, the floor gave way. Both officers were now standing; with only their upper bodies visible, as both fought to climb out of the hole they had created.

In all the negotiations that Pfaffenroth had been involved in this one had been the toughest. The usual good natured jokes amongst officers had not been present on this scene. Officers, were not even attempting to hide their fear and concern, behind false bravado.

Everyone was frustrated, with the lack of progress in the negotiations and seething with anger, at the fact, no one in command, seemed in a hurry to initiate a rescue.

Car 162: - **More screams coming now.**

"Mama, Mama..help me!"

Dispatcher: - **Advise more screams out.**

Oh God, help me please...

P-L-E-A-S-E...

CHAPTER 18
Siege Continues

The pain was constant. His head throbbed so badly that he had vomited. He had no feeling in his hands. He was so scared. Never in his life had he felt so alone. He stared at the ceiling through eyes that would not focus. He thanked God for the few minutes of respite from the beatings.

Please dear Lord do not forsake me. Make this never ending pain go away. I am so cold and so afraid. I wish I could be warm for just a few minutes. I hope someone will come get me soon. I hope Ray is okay. Ray, how did we get into this mess? I hope my wife won't worry too much about me. I know someone will come get me out of here. If I can just hold on for a few more minutes.

Why do they keep yelling at me? Why do they keep hurting me? I don't know what I could have done to them. I wonder if me and Ray could have done something different? They were laying for us. God, I am so cold. My head hurts. Please help me! Please, someone make them stop hurting me. I want to go home. I want to rest for just a little while.

What did they do to my leg? It really hurts. I can't stand the pain anymore! Why do they keep yelling at me about God and then hurt me? I can't feel my hands anymore. Why can't I move my hands or arms? Did they put my handcuffs on me? I wish I had something to drink. I just want to go to sleep.

Please mama, come get your little boy. Maybe someone will come get me. Anita, I miss you. I wish I could see you. God, don't let me die here. Come get me God. I don't want to die. Please come help me. Someone come and get me. I am so scared. I don't want to die like this. I'm not ready to die. Anita, I love you! Hey guys, please come get me. They keep hurting me. Make them stop hurting me. I feel sick to my stomach. Jesus, help me. My arms hurt. Did I get shot? Did Ray get out? Help me, somebody come get me. I am so scared. Oh, dear God, please deliver me from this place. I want to go home. Please help me. It hurts so badly. Please......

The two grim faced officers had been talking, while perched on top of the school, about the entire situation and what problems they thought needed to be corrected. The one with the binoculars scanned the front of the house while his partner began anew his complaints.

The negotiators were using tried and tested methods that had always worked for them in the past. None of them could get past the fact that this was not a typical incident.

The very fact that someone had been brazen enough or crazy enough to kidnap, beat and shoot police officers should have been enough evidence that it was time to think in another direction.

The second officer shook his head in agreement as he laid the binoculars down and rubbed his gloved hands together. The first officer coughed violently, then continued his monologue.

Throughout the entire ordeal one little thing had been overlooked. One little minor problem that needed to be attended to. Those people inside the school, calling the shots, forgot something. The fact the operation was being run by the book did not alleviate the problem, it simply masked what should have been the one and only true mission.

The one and only goal was and should be the rescuing of Hester, alive. It was probably little consolation to Bobby that the staff meetings were being held in an orderly fashion.

He probably didn't really care that the department had come up with some really wonderful intelligence information.

The second nodded his head again as he thought about what Hester must be going through.

Lying on that cold floor in that house Hester might be wondering why no one had come to get him yet. He might be praying that officers would soon rescue him.

Maybe Hester had stopped hoping for a miracle. Maybe the continuous beating he had to endure for hours prevented him from knowing what was going on.

Maybe the agony of relentless torture made him unable to do anything in his pain shrouded mind but pray for death. To pray for his God to come and rescue him.

As the hours ticked by, no one seemed prepared to initiate a rescue operation.

Mike Davidson, car 128 "Alpha", pulled up at Boxwood and Heard with his partner Phil Nason. Davidson had seen the news coverage and had come in early. He had chaffed at the bit, wanting to get to the scene as soon as possible, but had been forced to wait till midnight before leaving the precinct. Three months prior Davison had left the TACT unit after three years and went back to uniform patrol.

He and Nason had been assigned to traffic control at Boxwood and Heard but Davidson had immediately left and walked to the school. It didn't take him long to get involved as he stepped inside the school.

133

Melton(540): - **Can you send a uniform officer up in the back door of the apartment building where we are so we can tell him what we need.**
Randle(102): - **Check, stand by just a minute I will let you know who is coming, 102 to 104.**
Dispatcher: - **102 to 104.**

Summers(104): - **104, 102 go ahead.**

Randle: - **102 they need a uniform officer at the flagpole in front of the elementary school to take instructions from TACT Unit, 540. I need the name of the man coming.**
Summers: - **Alright.**
Summers: - **104 to 102.**
Randle: - **Go ahead 102.**
Summers: - **102, Mike Davidson is coming down, where do you want him to come to?**

Later Davidson would talk of listening to Hester being kicked and beaten followed by screams.

"It was hard to listen to, really hard." Davidson said.

Lt. Parker stared out the window of the school at the white house. He had relieved Crews on the radio at around 11:30pm and was still trying to get Lindberg to answer the phone.

Parker: - **Repeat it for me Lin, you cut it off, I couldn't hear it all.**
Lindberg: - **Your radio, you battery still there I didn't think you would have your..inaudible. mother fuckers out here with a battery that wouldn't last all night anyway. You know yall.. inaudible. you know God damn well..inaudible. you God damn mother fuckers when yall get ready mother fuckers do it.**
Parker: - **What harm is there talking on the telephone, Lin, can you answer that question for me?... Lin is everyone in the house**

okay? It isn't going to hurt a thing for you to talk to me on the radio, I'm just here to work with you, how about telling me whether or not everyone in the house is alright?
Lindberg: - **Everybody in here okay, cept me, I am shot through the arm.**

And so it went for the next two hours negotiators tried to induce Lindberg into talking to them on the phone. After three hours negotiators simply tried to get Lindberg to talk at all.

Parker: - **Lin is there anything I can do for you, how is the arm doing? What did you say? Does anyone in there need anything Lin? We have been trying to work with you all night Lin, you know I can help you, I got in touch with Mr. Morgan just like you asked me to, I have done everything you asked me to do, how about picking up the radio and talking to me Lin? Lin you know I have kept up my end of the bargain for you and now it is up to you. I need to talk to you on the radio, I can't talk to you unless you respond, I was talking to you earlier how about picking up the radio and talking to me no. I have some important information for you. Lin there is someone down the way here who wants to talk to you I can't put him on the radio until I can find out if you can hear him, would you please pick up the radio and talk to me.**

As the one sided radio conversations dragged on the TACT unit and uniform patrol kept up their vigil on the house. At approximately 2:00am the TACT unit cut the gas off to the house.

2:15am
Randle: - **102 to 104.**
Summers: - **104.**
Randle: - **Check 102, when is the last time you made a relief on the scope man?**

Summers: - **Captain, unknown whether made the relief, I think they sent someone down there to relieve Cunningham, my understanding he has been relieved but I don't know when they sent someone else down there to make a relief.**

Randle: - **Alright as of this time why don't you try to make it on the hour.**

Summers: - **Alright, what is the location of the one you want me to get a relief on?**

Randle: - **It will be the one in the front and the one in the rear.**

Dispatcher: - **542 do you need a relief?**

Melton: - **542 negative, I'm okay.**

Dispatcher: - **Okay.**

Car 565: - **565 to 502, tell Bernard the Red Cross wagon, they have prepared a big pot of stew, it is going to be ready in the about five minutes, we are going to carry it to C.P. and then planning on relieving alternate north.**

Unknown car: - **they are speaking too low of a voice to understand.**

Unknown car: - **spotlight from the t.v. people are lighting us up, have someone tell them to turn it off.**

Maxey(TACT liaison to negotiators): - **503 to 566.**

Maxey: - **Are you still in a position near the house where you can check to see if you can still hear the radio from inside.**

Car 566: - **Check.**

Maxey: - **Okay standby we are going to try it on the radio, see if you can read us.**

TACT officers had crawled up to the northwest window and tossed a phone into the house at the request of negotiators.

3:00am

Negotiators at one point had gotten Lindberg to put the phone on the hook and a call was made successfully into the house. His brother Macklin had spoken with him for several minutes asking him to surrender or let Hester go.

Macklin, at the urging of negotiators had asked Lindberg how the Hester was and could negotiators talk with him.

"Let the devils hear the other devil." Lindberg said.

"Help me, Help!" Hester screamed.

Everyone in the school office could hear Hester screaming and calling for help before the phone was disconnected.

At somewhere around 4:00am Dorothy Sanders and investigators had returned to the school with George David.

"When was the last time you saw Lindberg?" an investigator asked.

"Last week, I went by and picked up a hot water tank from his house." David replied.

David was questioned for several minutes and escorted to the office.

"I'm going to hold this police radio Mr. George. I am going to hold it and I am going to press the button and I want you to talk into it like you are talking on the telephone and I want you to try and get Lindberg to pick up the telephone, we got a telephone there but he won't pick it up on his end, but we understand he trusts you." Crews said.

"I hope he will." David said.

"Okay we will tell him who you are, talk very loud, right? Start." Crews said.

"Who am I calling?" David asked.

"Tell him Lindberg, tell him who you are." Crews said.

David: - **Lindberg, Lindberg, this is George, Lindberg, this is George. Lindberg, Lindberg.**

"Tell him to pick up the telephone." Crews said.

David: - **Pick up the telephone and talk with me.**

"Now let's see if he does." Crews commented.

Crews: - **Lindberg that was George he wants to talk to you on the telephone, I don't know if you could hear his voice or not. That is your good friend George he wants to talk to you how about picking up the telephone.**
David: - **Lindberg, Lindberg, this is George, pick up the telephone and talk with me.**

Officers lying near the house could hear several voices talking inside the house and called the negotiators on the car to car channel.

"Can you tell what they are arguing about?" Crews asked the TACT spotter.

After being told it was unknown what was being said Crews had replied.

"Alright, if he is not wanting to pick up the phone right now."

"They are listening to the radio George, this is Lindberg come on outside, can you do that? Tell him, Lindberg come on outside and talk with me." Crews asked.

David: - **Lindberg come on out and talk with me, I want to talk to you.**

"Do it again, tell Lindberg, pick-up the telephone." Crews whispered.

David: - **Lindberg pick up the telephone, this is George he wants to talk with you.**

Crews: -Lindberg, you know George is an elderly person looks like you could show him a little bit of respect by at least coming to the telephone and talking to him.

At approximately 5:45am Lt. Quinn and his section of TACT officers arrived at the scene. Since the first entry team had been on post for nine hours a relief team was assembled from Quinn's men.

The alternate assault team leader was Phil Hale, and his team would consist of Easley, Bartlett, Long and Filsinger.

As the TACT unit organized its second team the negotiators continued to talk with David.

"Can't we go over there? David asked.

"Oh hell yeah, done shot one policeman and got another one in the house, you can't go over there. Do you know Earl Thomas?" Crews asked.

"Who?" David asked.

"Earl Thomas, do you know Squeaky?" Crews asked.

"I think so." David replied.

"Do you know T.C.? Are they dangerous, are they roughish type people, Squeaky and T.C. in there." Crews asked.

"Has he always been a pretty good fella, George?" Crews asked.

"As far as I know he his." David replied.

"He wasn't ever a hoodlum or nothing like that, a gangster?" Crews asked.

"Not that I know of. He got sick up in the head once before, I went over there and talked to him, got him to the hospital." David said.

"How long have you known him?" Crews asked.

"About two or three years." David replied.

"Can you think of anything George to say that we haven't said, that might help him?" Crews asked.

"No." David replied.

"Well, we have been here since eight o'clock last night." Crews said.

"Well, I'll be..." David said.

"He has had that policeman in there all night." Crews said.

"I heard it on the news, on the television." David said.

"It is five thirty now. Say this is your friend, come on Lindberg, I can help you." Crews said.

"Yall don't want to kill him?" David asked.

"Oh no, no, no, no one is going to kill him.

"Help, somebody help me..."
"P-L-E-A-S-E..."

CHAPTER 19
Bullhorn

A t 5:00am on Wednesday, January the 12th, Officer Pfaffenroth, had made telephone contact with Lindberg.

Pfaffenroth, a native of Fond Du Lac, Wisconsin, had returned home from running errands, when he learned of the hostage situation. He had driven to the scene in his 78, Ford, Courier.

After a brief conversation, Sanders, had tried to hang the phone up. The line did not disconnect and negotiators were able to listen through the open line. The members inside the house could be heard cursing and arguing. To negotiators this could only mean that there was dissension amongst the members. Captain Lewis thought that the members would soon surrender.

"Good, good, real good. What did Maxey say about the man at the corner of the house?" Crews asked.

"He said they could hear him, so I don't know if the radio is where they are. They are so busy arguing with each other right now. I am sure the radio is on." a second negotiator said.

"Don (Captain Lewis), do you think we would be helping our self if we used the bullhorn or hurting our self?" Crews asked.

At approximately 5:30am, a brief conversation between TACT officers indicated they were preparing for the worst.

TACT officer: - **we have got,..are you close to the point of vacuum.**
TACT officer: - **I'm not there, negative I'm at c.p. If you want, I'll come over there.**
TACT officer: - **We need you here, unless...we got about 90 or 98.**
TACT officer: - **Meet me at security we got the sandbags.**
TACT officer: - **Get enough of them up here, however many you can space behind, just start carrying them and carry as many up there as you can, I don't want...**

Crews had moved to 2243 Shannon and begun using a bullhorn to talk to Lindberg.

Pfaffenroth made brief contact with Lindberg twice before he hung the phone up. During a brief period when the phone line was open Pfaffenroth heard a voice say "You think you know what to do? Then kill him."

"We can't get anything resolved like that, pick the telephone up and talk to us. Let somebody talk to us Lin, get on the telephone, what harm can that be? We don't need to be hollering at you with this loudspeaker Lin."
Crews said.

While Crews stayed on the bullhorn, Pfaffenroth and then Larkin used the phone to try to make contact with Lindberg.

At 7:00am Sgt. Crews heard Hester scream out from the window.
"Do what he said to do!" Hester said.
"That was Hester, that was Hester just hollered out the west side window, said do what he said to do, what he said to do, the east side, I'm sorry." Crews said.
Crews got on the bullhorn.

"Lindberg we don't know what you want. We have to talk to you on the telephone to do what you want us to do."

Director Holt and the command staff were advised of what Hester had said and of Crew's opinion that Hester had spoken in a strong, clear voice. With that and other information the command staff concluded that negotiations should continue.

Several minutes later Crews briefed relief negotiators inside 2243 Shannon.

"We need batteries for the north precinct radio and for the unitale also. Hester is between that window and this back room here and the back room drops off just a little bit and that is where they have their prayer meetings back in there. Hester came to the window a little while ago or came somewhere close to it and hollered, do whatever they tell you to do, he didn't sound distressed, he just hollered, it was a good sign to me. He is conscious and sounded good. I don't know what he has been through during the night but in any event, if you do have to go in, no one has ever come to that window. I have been here since five o'clock. When I first started talking on the bullhorn they did pick up the telephone, this one guy, Lindberg, you know about him, 48 year old, male, black, mental patient. Well now he is the leader of the group, he is the head of the group but he doesn't refer to himself as Jesus, no. They do a Bible prayer study and they got screwed up somewhere to smoke pot and they do that and they don't drink water and they don't eat pork and they fast a lot, he has been in TPH, he doesn't take his medication anymore. He ran his wife off a week ago, she hasn't been able to come back." Crews said.

Captain Lewis was contacted by Dr. John Downs in the early morning hours of the 12th. Downs was a psychiatrist who had treated Lindberg in the 1970's. He briefed Lewis on Lindberg and of his diagnosis of him.

Downs termed Lindberg as being paranoid with secondary depression. He had been foretelling the end of the world since 1973. Sanders believed himself to be Christ. He even claimed to have been killed by the police in 1975 and brought back to life by God. He referred to himself as Little Jesus and believed himself to be immortal.

Downs clarified to Lewis in saying that Lindberg was psychotic with prominent religious delusions. He said he would be available for further consultation if the police needed anything else. Before getting off the phone Lewis had asked Downs one more question.

"Doctor Downs, would you be willing to try and talk to Lindberg?" Lewis asked.

"In his present condition I do not think I would be of much help." Downs had replied.

Crews, at 2243 Shannon, called Larkin at the school.

"Jeff(Larkin), we have a telephone in this house, we just found it, let me give you this number in case you need to call us. We will give it a try, it looks like 278-2511, 278-2511. If we can get the cord to stay in it, holler at me on the radio when you are ready to start again." Crews said.

"Lindberg we are still with you. We are still counting on you Lindberg so are those people in there with you. We need you to pick up that telephone and talk to us now, you are the leader of that group you are obligated to pick up that telephone and talk to us Lindberg. There are some people who need to talk to you Lindberg, they don't want to shout over this bullhorn. They want to talk to you over the telephone, pick up the telephone Lindberg." Crews called out over the bullhorn.

Crews called the school command post by phone again and spoke with Larkin.

"Is the electricity still on in the suspect's house? Okay, thank you Jeff(Larkin). Clark(Dunlap), the electricity is still on over there. That is what you said isn't it Jeff, affirmative? Oh, it is off, is that what you are saying. The electricity is off; it is off, okay thank you. I was just passing that information on to Chief Williams. Someone wants to know Jeff, when the lights were last seen on in the suspect house, do you have any idea? I saw them on about daylight. About fifteen minutes after daylight the situation changed Clark, Clark that is fifteen minutes before daylight?" Crews said.

Crews called out to Lindberg again over the bullhorn before calling the command post again.

"There was a light burning in this window and it is not burning anymore so I assume the electricity is cut off." Crews said.

He turned to another negotiator while holding the phone with Larkin on the other end.

"Well the command post just told me the power was turned off, Herbie. When? Fifteen minutes before day light. Do you know who cut it off? Jeff, do you know how the power came to be turned off? The electricity particularly." Crews asked.

"Come on Lindberg, talk to me. There is no harm in talking Lindberg, you are supposed to be a leader. Well, leaders talk, so let's talk. We can work this thing out together and we can all go home. I know your neighbors are tired. Neighbors are telling us how much they like you, liked by all the people in the neighborhood, I know you want to keep that image, but we go to work this thing out together Lindberg. Lindberg, come on talk to me there is no harm in talking." Crews implored over the bullhorn.

Crews turned to Lewis.

"Captain Lewis, should we hit anything about religious leaders in the world that talk, communicate? Okay, we will stay away from that then, I was looking at the angle you know from religious leaders in the world talking, but yeah okay, we will stay away from that, yeah we don't want to do that then." Crews said.

Bleary eyed containment officers escorted negotiators back and forth from the school to 2243 Shannon while watching the house for movement.

Maxey: - **503 to Hotel 2.**
Maxey: - **503 to 502, 503 to 502.**
Pugh: - **Go ahead 503.**
Maxey: - **Got another negotiator coming over going to Hotel 2 will need someone to put him in position.**
Car 565: - **We are in the house back behind, clearing the window.**
Car 569: - **Saw movement in the back window, right hand side.**
Car 569: - **503, did you read me?**
Maxey: - **03 repeat.**
Dispatcher: - **569 saw movement in the rear window on his right side, rear window right side.**
Maxey: - **Southeast corner?**
Dispatcher: - **Be in the southeast corner, 503.**

9:15am
Pugh: - **502 to 540.**
Melton: - **40.**
Pugh: - **Are yall being relieved for breakfast?**

Melton: - **Haven't been relieved for breakfast as of yet.**
Pugh: - **Okay, we will see if we can get somebody up there to relieve you.**

Pugh: - **502 to 540.**

Melton: - **540 check.**

Pugh: - **Why don't you one at a time go to breakfast, just one at a time go.**

Melton: - **We are going to leave one scope man up here with a back up.**

Pugh: - **Check.**

Police Director Holt: - **1010 to 500.**

Captain Music: - **500 go ahead.**

Holt: - **Are you picking up any sound from the house at all?**

Music: - **500 we talked to negotiator, not picking up any sounds at this time.**

Holt: - **How long has it been since you had any contact with him?**

Pugh: - **502, Walter Crews said it was just after they was last contacted they heard.**

Car 562: - **We haven't heard any movement in the last,..almost three hours.**

Holt: - **1010.**

Car 546: - **46 to 503 did you read the kell set from the negotiator?**

Holt: - **1010, have you got the kell set on?**

Unknown car: - **It is on.**

Holt: - **1010 copy, we are reading the kell.**

A handwritten poster along with a Polaroid picture had been found attached to the oak tree in the front yard of 2239 Shannon. It had not been noticed during the night.

The sign, bearing the likeness of a pig's face above a message that read, Wanted for Murder Mr. Hog known aliases Pork, swine, hog, pig. Currently under investigation for first degree hypertension and other crimes against the health of mankind. Subject known to frequent greasy spoons and carry-out shops but can also be found in the best restaurants and homes. Approach at your own risk! - Subject is considered extremely dangerous.

The Polaroid picture that had been tacked up with the poster had been taken at night. No one could tell who the male was in the picture. There were two things about the picture that were easily recognizable.

The male in the picture had a uniform on.

He was a Memphis police officer.

CHAPTER 20

Silence

9:40am, January 12th, 1983

"Talk to me Lindberg, I want to help you... I couldn't understand what you said. Talk to me Lindberg I want to help you... I couldn't understand what you said. Talk to me Lindberg tell me what you said, I want to help you but you have got to tell me how I can help you." Larkin said over the bullhorn.

A few minutes before 10:00am Halloe Robinson the principle of Shannon Elementary School was escorted into the school and spoke with investigators.

For six years Robinson had seen Lindberg on several occasions but had never had a conversation with him, nor for that matter, ever been in close contact with him. At about 11:30am on January 11th Lindberg had left his house, walked across to the school and without comment gave Robinson several torn pages of scripture from the Bible. Lindberg then turned away and walked back into his house.

Robinson gave investigators the torn Bible pages.

"Lindberg repeated a couple of sentences to us, R.O. were unable to pick it up, how is the boom thing coming? a negotiator asked Lt. Parker over the phone.

"I'm coming over with the boom mike right now." Parker answered.

"Lindberg will you come over here by the window and talk to me so I can help you. I know you said something a few minutes ago but it wasn't loud enough, would you repeat it?" Larkin said over the bullhorn.

Negotiator on radio: - **Tell everyone to be perfectly quiet, tell everyone to be perfectly quiet, no talking. I can hear voices from the house. I can hear them moving something around.**

"Can we get a longer cord and set it closer to their window? Larkin asked.

Larkin: - **503, we can hear voices from within the house in normal talking conditions and we can hear movement without them trying to attract our attention or being excessive, if we had a longer cord we could get a better position and probably get even better sound than we have got now.**
Maxey: - **What part of the house do you hear them?**
Larkin: - **In the very back. We can be more positive about it if we could position our boom a little closer, we will be able to do that with the longer cord.**
Maxey: - **There is a broken window on the front porch.**
Larkin: - **Uh,.. we can't position ourselves to get to the broken window on the front porch we are dealing with a broken window on the side, near the den area, that is where we hear the voices.**

"Linberg can you hear me in there? Lindberg can you hear me in there? Lindberg come over and talk to me, come over here and talk to me so I can help you. I need to talk to you Lindberg. Will you come over here and talk to me, I want to help you but I can't help you if you won't let me." Larkin said over the bullhorn.

Larkin was relieved on the bullhorn by Shotwell.

"Hello, Lindberg, this is Shotwell with the hostage team. Lindberg is everything alright? We need to know you can give us a call or call you, put the phone on the hook, let us call you and see if everything is okay." Shotwell said.

"Is that smoke coming out of that air-conditioner? a negotiator asked.
"Yeah looks like it. They may have set a fire in there. Let me go out there and check it." second negotiator said.

"Lindberg, just holler out the window, do you need any blankets or something, just holler out the window and let us know, I hear you a little bit, what did you say? Lindberg do you need anything, any blankets to stay warm, just let me know something. Lindberg, let me know something man, it is getting cold out here and I am sure it is getting cold in there now you need to tell me something that you want." Shotwell said over the bullhorn.

It went on all morning, the negotiators talking and getting no response.

The TACT unit waited and listened and watched.

TACT officer: - **Okay, 510**(Sgt. James Bland), **go ahead and secure your position and when you get on top let me know.**
TACT 520: - **520 to 510 we are in position.**
Bland: - **Okay 510.**
Bland: - **510 to 30 are you on the roof?**
TACT 546: - **546 to 510 I have moved down to the very far west side of the upper roof.**
Bland: - **510, I'm at the house next door I can see you just pull.. inaudible..reach the button.**

Around 1:30pm the TACT unit continued to bring in equipment.

TACT 501: - **501 to 16 we are here at the corner of Boxwood.**
TACT 516: - **16 to 501 come back.**
TACT 501: - **The stuff requested from the (gun)range is on Boxwood, right at the corner.**
TACT 516: - **515 is going to meet you down there.**

Maxey: - **503 to 500.**
Music: - **500.**

Maxey: - **503, where do you need that light truck from the fire department.**
Music: - **500 to 503, set up at the school on the lot, if you can get it up there out of the way.**

1:59pm
Linda Houston called the police department saying she thought her brother Andrew was possibly inside the house. She said the group believed they could not die if the cause was right.

2:50pm
Air Unit: - **Air Six, a radio check please.**
Dispatcher: - **Check.**
Air Unit: - **This is the frequency, right?**
Dispatcher: - **Check Air Six.**

"Lindberg hang the phone up so we can talk to you, how do you like those Memphis State Tigers, they are number one, what do you think about Keith Lee, how do you like those Tiger Lindberg?" Shotwell said over the bullhorn.

"We are not picking up any sign of verbal response nor any sounds of movement." a negotiator said to another.

"Lindberg hang the phone up so we can talk to you. Your family is worried about you and your friends are worried about you. Don't put them through this. Meet us half way, we can talk about it. Give us some kind of sign. Let us know your are okay. Tap on the window or knock on the wall, just any kind of sign." Shotwell said over the bullhorn.

"No signs at all coming from next door." negotiator talking to another negotiator.

Unknown Car: - **We just had two motorcycles drive down the street.**
Dispatcher: - **Okay, are you on Shannon.**
Unknown Car: - **They just drove down Shannon on the street right in front of the house.**
Dispatcher: - **Okay.**
Bland: - **510 to scope man, advise your spotter to turn his hat around.**

Pugh: - **502 to 501, 515 is with Light, Gas and Water and the fire department.**

TACT 545: - **545 to 544.**

TACT 544: - **544.**

TACT 545: - **Okay 545 to 46 I need to meet with you and get the keys to the vehicle.**

TACT 544: - **Okay 545, can you meet me on the roof, the upper roof at the west side of the school.**

5:18pm

Melton: - **540 to 1080 I am at Kerr and Trezevant. I have a female, black, Verna Thomas, states she is a relative of Earl Thomas that she was in the building earlier today and requesting permission to come back in.**

Car 1080: - **Have somebody escort her down here, end door where the family is.**

5:40pm

Unknown Car: - **Traffic van to command post we are getting an orange colored light from the den, rear on the east side, appears to be maybe a fire burning...Come back command post do you read me?**

C.P.: - **Give me that location one more time.**

Unknown Car: - **East rear, an orange looking light, irregular, like maybe flames and it seems to be getting brighter as it goes.**

C.P.: - **Okay, 565.**

TACT 569: - **Okay 569, the fire, light appears to be coming from more of the center of the house, it's just glowing towards the right hand rear.**

C.P.: - **Okay is this the house in question, 569? 569 can you determine if it is the house in question?**

Unknown Car: - **500, do we start the fire equipment?**
Music: - **Negative, 500.**

5:47pm
TACT 545: - **Do we have a number on how many people we have in the house?**
TACT 563: - **563, I would say around four, correction that is five.**
TACT 545: - **Okay, we got five boxes coming.**

"I can see where you and I can have this to talk about cause we got a lot of things in common, now you have been over there and the last time we heard from you was two o'clock this afternoon, give me a chance to help you out. come on Lindberg lets show what a good leader you are man. We need good black leaders like you. Give me a chance to help you out man." Shotwell said over the bullhorn.

The sound of the amplified voice burst through the bullet holes in the windows, the words echoing throughout the house and long ago ignored by the men who lay on the floor, deep in their own thoughts, their warm breath turned white in the cold.

Charred remains of burnt furniture and newspaper smoldered on the floor of the den, a wisp of smoke floated up and across the ceiling before slowly seeping out the holes into the night air.

Overturned furniture lay about the house and the stench of blood and sweat permeated the air despite the freezing temperatures.

A black, leather jacket lay on the couch against the north wall of the living room its arms flailed out to the sides. A patch adorned each arm of the winter garment. The flag of the United

States of America affixed to the left arm. On the right arm was a circular patch with an eagle perched atop the words Justice and Protection. The wings of the eagle were outstretched and smeared with blood.

CHAPTER 21

Informant

January 12th, 1983
Approximately 6:30pm

Vidulich was inside the school when he received a radio call from the North Dispatcher, requesting that he call the North Precinct as soon as possible. Vidulich called and was told by Officer Billy Tucker that an informant had called and needed to talk to him about the people in the house.

"Where does he want to meet?" Vidulich asked.

"Firehouse # 6 on Thomas, he's there right now," Tucker answered.

Vidulich and Downen left the school and headed for the firehouse located in their ward.

After arriving, Vidulich walked inside and saw a familiar face sitting inside.

Germaine Johnson* had been arrested by Vidulich and Downen on several occasions. He was a known drug dealer in the area. The small time, southern, drug dealer began speaking with the big, yankee, cop.

He told Vidulich, that despite being arrested by him, he respected him for always treating him right and never being harsh to him. He explained to Vidulich, that he thought it was wrong, for the people in the house on Shannon to have done the things they had. He told Vidulich and Downen that there were at least three men who had escaped from the house that were over in Hurt Village.

Johnson was hustled to the cruiser and driven to Shannon Elementary. Vidulich gave his winter jacket to Johnson and told him to put the hood over his head as they got out and walked into the school.

Investigators interviewed Johnson before telling Vidulich to take him through Hurt Village and attempt to pick-up the men. Vidulich and Downen took Johnson to the North Precinct and picked up an undercover car.

Vidulich drove slowly around Hurt Village, with Downen in the passenger seat and Johnson slumped down in the back.

Johnson pointed at 620 N. Seventh.

"T.C. stay there with his mama in "B". He hurt his hip over at Berg's house. Pete and Hairy got out with him. Think maybe Hairy left town," Johnson said.

"Right there, 630, number "A", Hairy lived there. He got a brother that's fat," Johnson said.

Vidulich turned on to Thomas, hearing Johnson's voice coming from the back.

"There, 627, in "I", that's where Pete stay.

"Johnson, tell me what these guys look like?" Vidulich asked.

"T.C. is tall, bout your height, real skinny, dark, he got a chrome, .38 with a short barrel. Pete bout 30, maybe same height as Officer Winky," Johnson said while pointing at Downen.

Vidulich drove Johnson to a small side street off Thomas and Chelsea. Johnson was out of the car walking before it came to a stop. Vidulich and Downen made the block before pulling up at Chelsea and Thomas and stopping beside the three waiting cruisers. Inside the marked cars was Lt. Rodgers, car 105; Lt. William Oldham, car 106; Officers Woodruff and Colston, car 122, who were a two man car. The waiting men all knew what they were there for as Vidulich quickly outlined the locations that they were going to hit and who might be inside.

Approximately 8:08pm

The four cars pulled up near 620 N. Seventh Street # B and stopped. Oldham, Vidulich and Downen jogged to the front door as Rogers, Colston and Woodruff went around to the back. Vidulich knocked on the door which was quickly answered by a female holding a baby.

"Where's T.C.?" Vidulich asked.

"Here!" the man said as he limped from the back of the apartment to the front door.

The officers grabbed him and started handcuffing him.

"I was in the house, but I ran when the shooting started, I hurt my leg climbing over a fence, I swear to God!" T.C. said.

"Who are you ma'am?" Oldham asked the female.

"I'm T.C.'s wife, Charlene Smith," she answered back.

T.C., his wife and child were hustled out to Woodruff and Colston's car and placed in the back. Oldham stayed with the car.

8:14pm

The officers walked across the frozen ground towards 627 Thomas #I. Rogers, Vidulich and Woodruff took the front as Colston and Downen watched the back.

Vidulich knocked on the door.

"Who is it?" a female voice asked from inside.

"PO-LICE, open the door," Vidulich said.

Jenevia Murphy opened the door and stepped back allowing officers to come in.

"Who's that?" Vidulich asked pointing at the man sitting on the couch.

"Ricky Tucker," came the answer from the man.

"Where's Pete?" one of the officers asked.

"Don't know," Murphy answered.

After officers searched the apartment, Murphy and Tucker accompanied them back across Hurt Village and were put in a second car. All four cars headed out for the three minute drive to the old police headquarters building.

It was an imposing gray, stone building. Five stories high with a length and width covering one city block. You would have never heard anyone describe it as beautiful or sleek. It was functional, with a design that denoted strength and security.

The building was the perfect place, for the Memphis Police Department, to have called home. The city jail had been housed within the building. Male prisoners secured on the top floor and female inmates on the third floor. The remainder of the building had been occupied by the department's administration and investigative bureaus.

The building had stopped taking prisoners in 1981. The administration and bureaus had moved in 1982 to the ultra modern, 12 story Criminal Justice Center, at 201 Poplar. The two buildings were a block apart in downtown Memphis and within sight of the I-40 bridge into Arkansas.

Inmates were housed in the six floor, glamour slammer, that was attached to the east side of the Justice Center which was administrated by Shelby County, with the city leasing two floors, 11th and 12th, from the county. The administration and communications had the 12th floor and the investigative bureaus were on the 11th.

The old headquarters building, with its huge, marbled 1st floor and dirty beige carpet throughout, replaced by brown brick and red-clay colored carpet.

The stone gray building had one tenant remaining within its walls, Security Squad/IAB. These investigators handled all complaints against police officers and all police involved shootings.

Sgts. Collier and Landers of Security Squad and Sgt. Garner of the Violent Crimes Bureau sat in the Security Squad office waiting for the officers to arrive. Collier and Landers had been sent by Lt. Tusant, earlier to interview any witnesses or suspects that were located during the round-up. Lt. Wilson had told Garner to assist with the interviews.

The three investigators heard the approaching foot steps outside their office as the door opened with officers leading in the little group who were separated in different parts of the office while Vidulich talked to Landers, Collier and Garner.

Landers and Collier secured T.C. in an interview room as they began questioning him. Vidulich, Rogers, and Oldham stayed at Security Squad while Woodruff, Colston and Downen drove over to 630 N. Seventh #A to see if Hairy was home.

8:25pm

When the officers got to #A they spoke briefly with Betty Coleman.

"Ms. Coleman do you know a man named Hairy?" Downen asked.

"No, I don't know anyone by that name." Coleman answered.

"Ma'am we need everyone in the apartment to come into the living room." Downen asked.

Ms. Coleman walked to the foot of the stairs and called upstairs. Benjamin Coleman Sr., Benjamin Coleman Jr., Timothy Coleman, James Payne and Gregory Cole trudged down the stairs. The officers briefly spoke with the men, none claiming to know Hairy. Downen, Colston and Woodruff drove back to the headquarters building turning over the information on the five men to Landers and Collier.

While the three officers were gone Collier and Landers had been questioning Thomas Carter "T.C." Smith.

"T.C., when did you leave the house?" Collier asked.

"Man, I left when the shooting started." T.C. replied.

"Were you involved in the assault on any officers?" Collier asked.

"No, that weren't none of me." T.C. said.

"How did you hurt your leg?" Landers asked.

"Climbing over Lindberg's fence." T.C. answered.

"Who shot the officer T.C." Collier asked.

"I don't know I was running out the back when I heard the shooting," T.C. said.

"Who was in the house when you ran out the back?" Collier asked.

"Man, it was Lindberg, his son Larnell, Cassell Harris, Michael Coleman, Julius Riley, everybody call him "Red" and another dude named JuJu. T.C. said.

Collier and Landers questioned T.C. for close to an hour before walking out of the interview room to talk to waiting officers.

CHAPTER 22
Listening

At approximately 7:00pm on January 12th Holt held another staff meeting. Chief Inspector Cole, Chief Inspector Moore, Chief Inspector Warner, Chief Inspector Williams and Captain Lewis were in attendance. Holt told all present that the situation had not changed. Lewis asked that the electricity to the house be cut off. The request was granted.

Lt. Tusant ordered Sgt. Hollie to re-interview all family and friends of the members. Hollie walked to the east class room where they were housed. Hollie interviewed Dorothy Sanders again.

Dorothy said, most of the men she had seen come to the house, were from the Hurt Village Public Housing Project. The men would sit around and listen to Lindberg interpretations of the Bible. Dorothy said she didn't associate with any of the young men that came over, so she didn't really know any of their real names.

Linda Sanders, a daughter of Sanders, had arrived from New Mexico on the evening of the 11th. She told Hollie she had no idea why her father would take a policeman hostage. Linda had no information that would help the police.

Hollie spoke again with Albert Thomas, brother of Earl; Annie Thomas, sister of Earl; Jacklyn Jordan, wife of David Lee Jordan; Betty Jean Coleman, mother of Michael Coleman.

Coleman related to Hollie how police had come to her residence on Seventh Street looking for Michael. She said she didn't understand why Michael had hung up the phone on her son Ben.

The information Hollie obtained was compared with the information received from these people in previous interviews. It was hoped that something new might be learned.

Approximately 7:00pm
TACT car: - **513, if you can, we are another ten house up river, we are ready.**
Music: - **500 to 569 and 562.**
TACT 562: - **62.**
TACT 569: - **569.**
Music: - **Be advised we have L.G. and W. working, we are fixing to shut power off.**
TACT 513: - **Now there is going to be movement in front our house. Give us cover, give us some sign on the front window, and let us know if you see any movement at the front windows.**
TACT 513: - **Now.**
TACT 540: - **Check, no movement.**
TACT 513: - **540, did you say movement.**
TACT 540: - **Negative, no movement, no movement.**
TACT 513: - **We are fixing to begin.**

"Lindberg put the phone on the receiver and let me call you. Lindberg you been in there a long time man, are you ready to start talking to me, we haven't been able to get anything accomplished, now we can get a lot of things accomplished if you open the lines of communications, put the phone on the receiver and let me call you." Stepter said over the bullhorn.

"They are going to cut the power in about five minutes he said watch the house and see if there is any change and if there is any noise coming, keep steady talking on that thing." a negotiator whispered to Stepter.

"Lindberg you need to put the phone on the receiver so I can give you a call now I am standing by waiting for you to do it. I have been trying to figure out a way to help you out and you are not giving me any help on that." Stepter said over the bullhorn.

"Okay, start talking and don't stop." a negotiator told Stepter.
"Lindberg I just talked to your wife earlier man, she is worried about you and she is concerned about you and she is concerned about your well being now let us know how everything is going over there and let us know if you need any kind of medical attention or if you need any food, right now." Stepter said over the bullhorn.

Stepter talked continuously until a voice behind him whispered to him and into a phone.
"Okay, the power is cut, listen, see if you hear anything different," a voice from the negotiation command post said.
"The electricity has been cut but we don't hear anything more than we did. We have got the mike aimed out the side window, we haven't heard anything at all. No movement at all from the house that we can tell," the negotiator at 2243 said.

Approximately 7:35pm

C.P.: - **C.P. to 540, is the light yall want out at the corner of the school?**

TACT 540: - **Can you get, take a butt of a rock and knock that light out?**

TACT 521: - **521 to 513, the lights you wanted out have been turned off already, that is on at the back of the north side of the parking lot.**

TACT 565: - **565, we wanted a light out on a house west of that location and also the biggest thing is the cars with real bright lights shining all across these backyards.**

Unknown TACT: - **..to 540 only problem is turned out a lot of houses over there that can't stay out all night.**

TACT 565: - **565 to command post, the light from the news van down there are causing a bad glare across the back of this house, we need them cut.**

C.P.: - **Okay, C.P.**

Music: - **500 to C.P., I will take care of that I am over here.**

Music: - **500 to the officers at the intersection, east of the school.**

TACT 515: - **Tell 500, 515.**

Music: - **Advise the media they will have to turn those lights out. They have to turn those lights out.**

Quinn: - **501 to 568.**

Summers: - **68.**

Quinn: - **501, C.R.** (Summers) **can you read the license number on the maroon car parked in front?**

Bland: - **510 we have already got two of those sierra marbles over here, we are going to need some more, he will know what we are talking about.**

Bland: - **510 to 520.**

TACT 520: - **520.**

Bland: - **510, do you have a night view diversion in the vehicle?**

Quinn: - **501 repeat.**
Summers: - **Bravo-November-Victor, 5-2-0.** (tag on maroon car)
Quinn: - **Okay 501.**

Sometime around 8:00pm, an employee with C B S television, consented to let members of the TACT unit, use a parabolic microphone, which was placed at the southeast corner of the house, slipped through a bullet hole in the window by TACT officer Gallo. It was hoped that the microphone would pick up voices from within the house.

At about 8:20pm in the evening Pfaffenroth began looking for a place to catch a quick nap. He located a bean bag chair in an empty class room and promptly fell asleep.

An hour or so later Director Holt and several commanders of the TACT unit and Uniform Patrol stood outside the school. One of the TACT commanders requested a meeting with Holt in private.

The group walked into the school looking for a room to hold their meeting. The only room large enough, was the room where Pfaffenroth lay, in peaceful slumber. At Holt's direction, one of the commanders slid Pfaffenroth underneath a table. Pfaffenroth never stirred. The meeting began and became quite animated.

The facade of gentile, boardroom manners, and showing respect for a supervisory official quickly collapsed, into a full scale shouting match. A red faced Holt and at least one TACT commander screamed obscenities at one another. Holt would not budge from his decision not to order an entry. TACT and Uniform commanders protested that it was the only option left.

It was at some point during the meeting, that Pfaffenroth was finally awakened, by the emotionally charged meeting. Pfaffenroth began to stir and climbed out from underneath the table. The room that seconds before had echoed with shouts and curses, now resounded with roars of laughter at the sight of Pfaffenroth staggering to his feet.

"We have been here quite a while, come on Lindberg, help us out, meet us half way. Show us what kind of person you can really be, we all have been told how good you are, all you got to do is show us, it doesn't take much, just a little communication that is all it takes, please hang the phone up Lindberg." Stepter said over the bullhorn.

"Still no movement or sound. Cannot hear anything," a negotiator said over the phone.

The negotiators reported that they had been unable to establish any meaningful two way communication with Sanders or anyone else in the house.

Considering the length of time that had past this was deemed to be highly unusual. Lindberg would not talk over the phone. The police were totally blind as to what was going on inside the house. This was not a true hostage situation. The hostage takers were not making demands. The passage of time seemed to be working against negotiators. Some of the negotiators were wondering why Holt, had not given the green light, to the TACT unit.

Officers within the department took sides as to who to blame for the delay in rescuing Hester. Some blamed Holt, while others, pointed the finger at Mayor Hackett. The rumor that a TACT commander had flung a chair, in the general direction of the Mayor or the Director, or both, was being passed along.

The rumor solidified when it was announced, that since the chair had missed, the TACT commander must have only been firing a warning shot. Everyone knew the TACT unit never missed.

Hester had now been held hostage for almost twenty-four hours. No one knew for certain if he was even still alive. The last confirmed sighting of Bobby, had been earlier in the morning. Lindberg, having finally relented to repeated requests, had held Hester up in front of the window, in the northeast bedroom. That had been over twelve hours ago.

TACT unit officers had now been on station for almost twenty-two hours. Some uniform officers had not been to sleep for over thirty-six hours. No one wanted to rest until the job was done. No one present could get the voice out of their mind.

Dirty, sweat stained, uniforms clung to the bodies of tired officers. Fatigue and cold weather took its toll on already frayed nerves. Simple tasks, performed without thought earlier, now required more time. The fog of exhaustion began to shroud minds and numb reflexes.

The situation had passed mind numbing and was fast approaching unbearable.

"Talk loud and fast on that bullhorn alright? a negotiator said.

"Okay, let us know when." second negotiator said.

"If you get tired I will start on this one. There is going to be movement at rear of house, stay away. Will be movement at the rear of the house," a negotiator said.

"Lindberg listen to me, I want to talk to you Lindberg. Come on now we are going to have to do some talking..inaudible whatever you want all you have got to do is talk, we have not been able to talk to you in a while, you have got to talk to us, the friends and your family, you brother they are all worried about you." Stepter said over the bullhorn.

"Okay, slow it down just a little bit, stop and let us listen for a little while. Just slow it down," a negotiator told Stepter.

"Lindberg if you need some batteries for your radio let us know, we will throw them to you or get them to you some kind of way. If your phone is not working let us know that. We can get you another phone in there if you want to talk to us." Stepter said over the bullhorn.

TACT 513: - **513 to 545.**
TACT 545: - **545, go ahead.**
TACT 513: - **Tell negotiators to slow it down and quit for just a minute let us see if we can pick up anything.**
Maxey: - **503, do you want to slow it down or stop it?**
TACT 513: - **Stop for just a minute.**

"Hold it, they said to quit for a while. They are going to see if they can pick anything up with that mike," a negotiator said.
"Okay." Stepter said.

Approximately 10:00pm
TACT Car: - **...to 562.**
TACT 562: - **62.**
TACT Car: - **Leave your position and go over to the school and meet Officer Watson some place over there so yall can exchange vests.**
TACT 562: - **562 to 564**(Watson) **if you want to swap 16's** (M-16 military assault rifle) **bring it also.**

CHAPTER 23

Members Interviewed

January 12th, 1983
Approximately 8:50pm - Security Squad Office

Sgt Garner began talking to Jenevia Murphy.

"What is Pete's real name?" Garner asked.

"James Pete Murphy," Murphy said.

"How long have you two been married?" Garner asked.

"Five years," Murphy answered.

"When was the last time you saw him?" Garner asked.

"Pete and Squeaky left from over my place between seven and eight this evening," Murphy answered.

"What's Squeaky's real name?" Garner asked.

"Reginald McCray," Murphy replied.

"Did they leave in a car?" Garner asked.

"Yea, they left in Pete's 72, Mercury, it's a blue, four-door, Marquis," Murphy said.

"Where was he yesterday?" Garner asked.

"He left the house yesterday about 1:00pm and came back a little before 9:00 in the evening and we seen on the news about the shot police officer. We woke up this morning and he took me to the dentist about noon and when he picked me up Squeaky was with him," Murphy said.

"How did Pete hurt his leg?" Garner asked.

"I don't know, his leg wasn't hurting none when he came home last night," Murphy replied.

"Do you know who's in the house with Lindberg?" Garner asked.

"Cassell Harris must still be in the house cause his girlfriend Annette told me she had talked with him," Murphy said.

"How does Pete know Lindberg?" Garner asked.

"Pete went to school with his son Larnell. I only been over there once but I don't associate with Lindberg or any of Pete's friends. They have got some strange beliefs when it comes to religion and Pete don't like police cause they pushed him around when they arrested him for child support last year," Murphy answered.

"Does Pete have a gun?" Garner asked.

"Pete don't have no gun and he don't believe in violence," Murphy said.

"Where do you think Pete is right now?" Garner asked.

"Don't know, but wouldn't surprise me if he didn't try to go over on Shannon and get with Lindberg," Murphy said.

Garner stood up and escorted Murphy out of the interview room back into the office. He walked over to a phone and called the command post relaying the description of Pete, Squeaky and the blue car.

9:39pm

Garner sat down heavily in an interview room chair, rubbing his eyes as he began asking questions.

"Charlene, has T.C. ever been arrested?" Garner asked.

"Yea, he got picked up in 76 for assault to murder, he was tussling with some other dude, he did four months in jail," Smith said.

"Do you know Lindberg Sanders?" Garner asked.

"Don't know cept I know T.C. and some others from Hurt Village go over there to read the Bible," Smith said.

"Where was T.C. today?" Garner asked.

"He was with me all day," Smith answered.

"How about yesterday?" Garner asked.

"He left bout 9 in the morning and come back before the sun was all the way down," Smith said.

"Did he leave in a car or was he walking?" Garner asked, sensing that Smith was lying.

"He drove off in his burgundy, Buick," Smith said.

"When he came home did he have his car?" Garner asked, knowing that T.C.'s car was still parked in front of Lindberg's house.

"Naw, he come in telling me he had lost the keys," Smith said.

"Where did he leave the car parked?" Garner asked.

"Well,..I don't remember where he said it was," Smith said.

"Do you have a key for the car?" Garner asked.

"Yea," Smith said.

"Why didn't you and T.C. go get the car?" Garner asked.

"I don't remember why we didn't, we was gonna get it tomorrow," Smith said.

Garner gave up, he knew he was spinning his wheels asking any questions regarding T.C.'s involvement over on Shannon and listening to lies.

"How long has T.C. known Lindberg?" Garner asked.

"Been about five years," Smith said.

"What do they do over there at Lindberg's house?" Garner asked.

"T.C. don't tell me bout his business, all I know is they sit around and read the Bible," Smith said.

Garner chuckled as he stood up and escorted Smith out of the interview room and had her sit in the office.

10:25pm
Garner scratched his head as he looked over at Rick Tucker.
"Okay, Rick how do you know Pete?" Garner asked.
"Well, he was dating Jenevia then they got married," Tucker said.
"You ever been to Lindberg's house over in Hollywood?" Garner asked.
"Yea, Pete took me over there once, been over a year ago, Tucker said.

"You weren't over there yesterday?" Garner asked as he watched Tucker out of the corner of his eyes.
"No, no, I ain't been around there in a year or more," Tucker answered.

Garner turned his head as someone knocked then opened the interview room door. He saw one of the officers motioning him to come out in the office. He left the interview room and learned that communications was on the phone and needed to talk to him.
Garner immediately began writing on his pad as the senior dispatcher relayed the information to him.

10:45pm
T.C.'s mother, Bernice Smith had called communications wanting to speak with investigators about her son. A dispatcher had immediately taken her name, address and phone number

and told her someone would call her right back. Within two minutes the senior dispatcher had been on the phone with Garner.

Garner sat back in his chair as he listened to the phone ring. When the elderly female voice answered the phone Garner sat up in his seat. Smith told Garner that T.C. had been over at the house on Shannon when the fighting started but had run out when everybody got to shooting. He had hurt himself jumping over fences while running away. He had called her at home and she had picked him up at either Claybrook or Clayton, she couldn't remember which.

Garner thanked Smith for calling as he looked up and saw Collier and Landers coming out of the interview room. Garner saw T.C. sitting with his elbows on the table of the interview room his face buried in his hands.

"I need some of you uniformed officers to write up an arrest ticket on T.C. Take him to the jail and put a hold on him for two counts of assault to murder on police officers and make sure the jail gives you his clothes and tag'em in the property room," Landers said.

Approximately 11:25pm

Communications had called Garner again and told him that a lady had called about some men who were involved in the shooting of the police officer. Garner listened to the information and told communications to send cars over there and bring all the males to the Security Squad office.

Garner called and spoke with Shirley Crawley who lived over in Hurt Village. She said there were several black men sitting in an apartment near her reading the Bible and talking about who shot the police officer.

11:43pm

A half dozen officers came into the Security Squad office with five males, Ray Atkins, James Payne, Lee Rogers, Benjamin Coleman Jr. and Timothy Coleman.

Atkins told investigators that he had never been to Lindberg's house and had never met him. He didn't know anything about any religious cult.

Payne was interviewed and said he had been to Lindberg's house about two weeks ago with Tim Coleman. After several minutes of talking with Payne, investigators decided that because he was apparently illiterate and had some type of mental disorder the questioning ended.

Rogers was questioned but like Payne, investigators determined he too was mentally impaired and his interview ended as abruptly as Payne's did.

Tim Coleman told investigators that he had been to Lindberg's house on several occasions to study the Bible but he had not been there on the 11th of January. He did say he felt sure that his brother Michael was in the house.

Investigators spoke with Ben and after interviewing him for several minutes decided to take a taped statement from him.

1:00am January 13th, 1983

Collier and Landers sat across the table from Ben Coleman with a tape recorder sitting between them.

(In the following statement some questions and answers were removed for brevity. What is reprinted is the actual text from the statement).

Q: Benjamin, as you know prior to taking this taped statement from you we have discussed your brother, Michael Coleman being involved in the hostage situation on Shannon Street. Is that correct?

A: Um-hum...yea, yea.

Q: Is it your belief that Michael is out there in the house at 2239 Shannon with Lindberg Sanders?
A: I don't know. I don't know that.
Q: Do you think there's a strong possibility that he might be?
A: Might, might not.
Q: On Tuesday evening, about 8:30pm, did two policemen come to your home accompanied by a male, black and accuse Michael of stealing a purse?
A: Right.
Q: Would you explain just exactly what happened down there?
A: Okay,...they knocked on the door and my mother let them in and he asked for Michael Coleman. I said Michael Coleman is not here and he said something about Mike had stole a purse. I wanted to know where he could be located, you know. So I called a friends's house and he wasn't there. He talked to the guy who accused Michael of stealing and the phone was hung up. The guy left and I told the guy before he left that he had told a lie. Michael couldn't have stole anything. It was impossible for him to steal anything and he left. That was all that was said. The next thing I knew was a car was coming to Lindberg Sanders house.
Q: You said you called a friend's house to see if Michael was there. Who was the friends's house you called?
A: I called Lindberg.
Q: That's out on Shannon, is that correct?
A: Um-hum.

Q: Did you get to talk to Michael when you called out there?
A: No.
Q: Do you know who you talked to when you called out there?
A: No.

Q: Was there loud music playing when you called out there?

A: There was music playing.

Q: Okay, Did your mother call out there to see if Michael was out there?

A: I left the room on that. But I heard some argument and I didn't pay any attention to that. I really didn't know what the argument was about. I just heard some argument. I didn't pay any attention to that. But I do know that the guy that came in there, he looked like he was telling a lie.

Q: You're talking about the one that was accusing Michael of stealing a purse?

A: Um-hum. Funny type anyway.

Q: Have you seen Michael since Tuesday night?

A: No.

Q: Do you know whether or not your mother has seen Michael since Tuesday night?

A: No, she hadn't seen him either.

Q: Do you know whether she's talked to him since Tuesday night?

A: Umm...I don't know.

Q: Have you talked with him since Tuesday night?

A: She hadn't told anything about Michael.

Q: Do you think that Michael, correction. Disregard that. Tonight when the policeman picked you up to bring you up to this office where was you at?

A: I was over to a friend's house and...

Q: Who is this friend?

A: I call him Red, I don't know his real name. He's got a baby by my cousin.

Q: Is it Ray Aiken's house?

A: Ray...yea, it's Ray.

The questioning continued from Collier and Landers.

Q: Who is your friend?
A: T.C.
Q: What did you'all do after you went out there?
A: Smoke a little reefer.
Q: Are you a frequent visitor to Berg's house?
A: Yes, I'd get out there as much as I could.

Several questions later investigators came back to the topic of the hostage situation.

Q: Do you know what caused the problem that's going on out there now?
A: Yes.
Q: Alright, what caused the problem?
A: The guy that accused Michael of snatching a purse.
Q: Okay, have you talked to anybody that was at Berg's house that night, do you know what caused the problem out there?
A: Evidently, had to barge in, I don't know if they had a warrant or not. I wouldn't know that. But,...it...they went in there. If the police had been polite, then I know he would have been polite. You know.
Q: Okay, have you talked to anybody that was at Berg's house the night that all of this started?
A: I talked to somebody, but I don't know who he was. That's what I'm saying. I don't know who it was. It wasn't...when I called, I asked to see if Michael was there. Okay, somebody said yes, somebody said no. I took it as he was there and if they wanted to go there, I would have brought them there. They said no, that's okay. They didn't want to go out there, then turned around and

I'm watching television and here go something about the police being over there. They...it was all over this person, over this guy. Started the whole thing.

The statement ended shortly after. All five men were released and four of the five declined offers to be driven home, the fifth, Ben Coleman asked for a ride.

Landers, Collier and Garner drove back to Shannon Elementary School arriving at somewhere around 2:15am.

CHAPTER 24

Bugged

At approximately 10:15pm Sgt. J.C. Kellum of the Organized Crime Unit arrived at the school and was meet by Lt. Hank Thomas, his supervisor. Thomas had called Kellum earlier at home and asked him about a power amplification type microphone system.

After confirming O.C.U. did have one Kellum was told to get it and come to Shannon Elementary School. He had driven to Captain Talley's house and picked the mike up before heading to the school.

Thomas had been home recuperating from a broken arm when he had been called and asked to come in by Captain Lewis. He had cinched his broken arm up tight and driven to the command post.

At 10:30pm Kellum and Thomas spoke with Chief Warner who told the officers that there had been no sound or movement detected since 6:00pm and the power mike would be needed to confirm if anyone was still alive in the house.

Kellum was taken by TACT officers to 2243 Shannon and shown where the CBS mike had been placed on the east side of the target house. He was then taken to 2237 Shannon where Officer Gallo crawled to 2239 Shannon and dropped another mike through a bullet hole in a window on the northwest side (living room) and then ran line back to the 2237 address where Kellum hooked the line to the power mike system.

Kellum was told to monitor for any sounds and to notify the command post if any were detected.

Approximately 10:50pm

"Lindberg, hey that matter about the warrant, we have already resolved that it was a mistake, we have resolved, come on and let us talk to you. Why don't yall come on out, let us talk to you, give us a call, everything is okay we have already resolved the matter but we need to talk to you first, give us some kind of signal, let us know that you understand," Shotwell said over the bullhorn.

"Hush up, who is that talking to him? Did you hear anything?" one negotiator asked another.

"No," the second negotiator said.

"Have they got him on the phone?" first negotiator asked.

TACT 515: - **515, negotiators advise they cannot hear him.**

"How is the police officer doing? Come to the side window," Shotwell said over the bullhorn.

"Shotwell, holler louder, and pause longer between..Okay," a negotiator said.

"Lindberg, how is the police officer doing? We can't hear you. Lindberg, I can't understand you," Shotwell said over the bullhorn.

"Tell Shotwell, do not use the word police officer, that is what set him off," a negotiator said.

"Did Lewis say that?" second negotiator asked.

"No, this was a special request by the TACT officers," the first negotiator answered.

"Okay, we were not aware of it at this point. Go ahead. we have got to find out about the officer," the second negotiator said.

"Lindberg, we can't hear you? How is the police officer doing? How is everybody doing in there? Lindberg, we still can't understand you, you are going to have to come to the window, we can't understand you," Shotwell said over the bullhorn.

"Hold it, he is talking but I can't hear. I hear an echo type voice," a negotiator said.

Kellum immediately detected a male voice he recognized as being Lindberg's. The voice was coming from the middle part of the house (den) and got louder as he walked to the living room and then would grow lower as he paced about the house.

"God won't let this happen, these no good mother fucking pigs," Lindberg said.

"Yall, want to do the right thing, you lied, you mother fuckers, lying mother fuckers. Lying pigs started this shit, accuse me of stealing mother fucking purse. Want me to cooperate do they, I'll cooperate, the mother fuckers, gonna give them something the fuckers been wanting but they ain't gonna like the shape it in when they get it," Lindberg said.

"You hear me mother fucking pig your gonna die and all the pigs outside are gonna die! Do you hear me fucking..., you mother fucking pig, blink your eyes if you hear me mother fucker," Lindberg said.

TACT Car: - **Let me know when Charles is in place with yall.**
TACT 549: - **549 to 513 I am moving around that way right now.**
C.P.: - **Air 7.**
Air 7: - **Air 7.**
C.P.: - **Contact the command post for Air 51.**

11:30pm
Unknown Car: - **Everything quiet in that house, tell the negotiators to start negotiating on their bullhorn.**
Music: - **500, Okay, is there any reason that Hank Thomas or Kellum see for not coming into negotiations from that vantage point.**
TACT 549: - **49 to 500.**
Music: - **Go.**
TACT 549: - **They advise they have no qualm for starting the negotiations, they advise it would be helpful.**
TACT C.P.: - **Okay, this side had rather they not start right now, it will be discontinued for a while, the TACT C.P. to Negotiation C.P. did you read that.**
TACT C.P.: - **Fred,..Adair ask about starting back the negotiations it is in consensus right now whether to hold off for a few minutes right now, we will let you know.**

"Your bleeding mother fucker..lying mother fucker, God damn you,.. you fucking pigs," Lindberg said.

January 13th, 1983
Approximately 12:10am
"Lindberg is everything okay? Lindberg you are going to have to speak up a little louder I can't understand you," Negotiator said over bullhorn.

"Lying pigs always wanting me to do something for them, mother fucking pigs..you think I'm a damn fool, I..what you gonna do, you gonna throw some gas on my ass,..I know..well mother fucking pigs my water still working, I just wash that shit off me," Lindberg said.

"God damn you pigs,..click, click, click, lying pigs," Lindberg said as he cocked and un-cocked a pistol.

Unknown Car: - **Dispatcher, advise all the cars that are going to their positions they will have to go around because we have a pumper blocking the street and it cannot back up enough for anybody to get by.**

TACT 515: - **Tell negotiators that the man is trying to talk to them.**
Unknown Car: - **515, negotiators are trying to reach him now.**
TACT 513: - **513 to 515 tell negotiators every time he tries to talk, they are cutting him out.**
TACT 513: - **513 to 515 tell negotiators to ask how the police officer is?**
TACT 515: - **Check.**
Unknown Car: - **515, tell the negotiators to listen to what he is trying to say. Quit negotiating and listen.**
TACT 515: - **515, Check.**
Unknown Car: - **515, ask them to ask about the police officer again.**
TACT 513: - **Have the negotiators to ask him if they will bring the police officer to the window where they can talk to him.**
TACT 515: - **Negative, from up here to command post.**

"Lindberg we are trying to understand you, you have got to come to the east side of the house, please speak up a little louder," Negotiator said over the bullhorn.

"My brother is dead, my dad is dead, God is dead, the devil is dead and this son-of-bitch don't have no air in him either," Lindberg hissed.

CHAPTER 25
Preparations

"I'm cold, I'm cold, I'm cold, I'm cold, I'm cold man, I'm cold," Lindberg cried as he walked to the bathroom and threw up.

"Yeah, we are getting some sound," the negotiator told a second negotiator.

"Hold it, it is cold, he said it is cold, is cold man, it is cold, he stopped now," the negotiator said.

"Lindberg, I told you earlier I am here to help you. Put down your weapons we are going to supply you with some heat, just let us know when you are ready, Lindberg, we have got a warm place for you." Douglas said over the bull horn.

"He is crying saying I am cold, over and over. Yeah that is what we are gong to play on, alright get on the bullhorn, he is cold and crying," a negotiator told Douglas.

"Lindberg, we have some warm blankets and some heat, there is no sense in going on and being cold. I told you I am here to help you," Douglas said over the bull horn.

Dispatcher: - **Okay, we have one up on the traffic frequency now, we have one using radio on traffic frequency now, advise the negotiators.**

"We got him on the traffic frequency that is channel eight. Okay," Negotiator said into the phone.

Unknown Car: - **Advise a guy from the Commercial Appeal here, advise he is supposed to replace one of the newspaper people at Boxwood and Shannon.**
Unknown Car: - **He will have to go around the perimeter to go over there.**

Sometime around 1:00am on January 13th Holt held another staff meeting. All the principal division heads were there along with Captain Music and Lt. Thomas.

Thomas gave a summation to the assembled group about the boom mike monitoring. He told all present that the situation, in his estimation, was becoming more dangerous. He said that someone in the house was coughing heavily and the sounds of someone vomiting had been heard. The entire command staff, by now, knew that the members did not believe in receiving medical treatment.

Everyone was also aware that Lindberg had been shot and Hester had been beaten badly. It was also felt that other persons in the house had most probably been injured. The staff discussed the following topics, Was Hester alive or dead? Were other persons injured other than Sanders?, Would a further delay result in Hester's death or contribute to the death of other persons in the house? and finally, although negotiations had failed and no meaningful dialogue had been established, should the negotiations continue?

The command staff began discussing tactical solutions and felt that there were two options open.

Option one, was the introduction of tear gas into the house with the hope that it would force the occupants out.

Option two, a tactical entry in conjunction with the use of gas.

The command staff considered the probability of serious and fatal injuries versus maximum personal safety. It was decided that the only viable option would be a tactical assault in conjunction with the introduction of gas, flash bangs and sound simulators. Those in attendance decided that any further delay would likely result in the death of those persons who were injured.

On January 13th, somewhere around 2:35am the order to assault the house was given to the TACT unit. The primary objective would be to gain entry, locate Hester and move him to safety. The secondary objective would be the removal of all other injured persons and the arrest of all perpetrators.

The negotiators inside 2243 Shannon received a phone call about 2:40am and told to discontinue all negotiations and report back to the main command post at the school.

At this time negotiating attempts ended in preparation for assault, was the final entry in the negotiators log book.

Director Holt, Captain Jim Music and several chiefs were present, in the library, for the briefing of the entry team.

Some were coughing from extended time outside, others couldn't seem to warm up, even when they came inside. One TACT officer still on the roof had actually lost the hearing in one ear, from the ear piece, he had worn for too many hours.

The primary objectives were to gain entry, locate Hester and move him to safety, as expeditiously, as possible. The secondary objective would be the removal of all other injured persons and the arrest of all suspects.

The primary assault team was given the latest intelligence on the occupants in the house.

Hester was presumed badly injured and was located somewhere in the north, northeast side of the house. It was also presumed, that Hester, would not be able to walk out under his own power. Lindberg Sanders and possibly others, in the house, had been shot or injured.

There was no hard data on the number of weapons available. It was known that both officer's revolvers and ammo had been seized by the suspects. The officers were reminded that Sanders was reported to have a large collection of hunting rifles and shotguns. A rough outline of the house had been drawn up but was not considered reliable. The number of occupants was estimated to be approximately seven to twelve males and possibly one female.

All power to the house, both electrical and gas, had been cut off. Presumably, this would mean, all those in the house, would be slow to react after entry was made, due to the cold temperatures.

The TACT unit plan was simple and direct. The six man entry team, would move in pairs, once the rear door was breached. The first two would head to the nearest defendable portion of the house. They would then provide cover for the next two. The final pair, would cover the rear door, to allow an escape route, in case something went wrong.

The entire group would then move north through the house, locate Hester and take him out the front door. Two officers would carry Hester, two would cover the evacuation and two would maintain control of the front door and the area near the front door.

Once Hester was rescued, objective number one, would be completed. The members would then leap frog, back through the house and carry out objective number two.

If at any point, during the operation, a team member went down, he would be evacuated by one to two members, while the others provided cover by fire. Officers from the secondary team would move in to replace those injured.

TACT officers had scrounged around, looking for extra bullet resistant vests, to put on under the entry vest they would be wearing. No one wanted to think about the damage that could be done, if any one officer, took a round from a hunting rifle, at close quarters.

The officers would be going in wearing gas masks, assault helmets, a Level II vest underneath a Level III vest which weighed close to seventy-five pounds and plenty of ammo.

McNair, the thirty-four old team leader, had thirteen years on the job. The make-up of the team he would be going in with had changed since he had first arrived over twenty-seven hours ago.

Rutherford the thirteen year veteran, known for his tactical skills and Ray, the former construction worker, were still on the team. R.O. Watson, like Ray, a shotgun expert, had been added to the team. C.R. Summers had replaced Todd, who had a sinus infection and had difficulty breathing with a gas mask on. D. Hubbard was given Dawkins' slot because of his enormous physical strength.

None of the six members had less than twelve years of experience on the job with Rutherford being the rookie with over twelve and a half years. All were thirty-four years old except Summers who was the old man at thirty-six. Rutherford had driven a bus before coming on the job, while Summers had left IBM. Watson, the Vietnam war veteran, had left military service and joined the department.

Summers had been given a handcuff key to be used to free Hester's arms. A set of bolt cutters would be placed at the front door just prior to the assault in case the handcuff key didn't work.

Captain Music and Lt. Pugh were going stay at the TACT command post at 2247 Shannon. Lt. Quinn was to handle front security and insure an orderly transfer from tactical to investigatory once the situation was stabilized in the house. Lt. Maxey was assigned rear security with the same responsibilities as his counterpart in the front. Maxey was told by Music to utilize remaining TACT personnel, not already with an assignment, to whatever role he deemed necessary.

Sgts. Fields, Bland and Huff were to be the inner perimeter team leaders to provide whatever immediate logistical support the assault team needed in the form of manpower, equipment or medical aid. The three Sergeants and the TACT officers under their command were responsible for initiating the assault with the introduction of C.S. gas, flash bangs and artillery simulators into the house.

All around the little white house heavily armed TACT personnel waited.

On the roof of the school covering the front were TACT officers, J. Bailey, .308 caliber bolt and scope; Melton,.223 rifle; E. Lancaster, .223 rifle; and Jeter with his .223 bolt and scope. Their cover men on the roof were Cheslock and Thurman who were both armed with M-16s.

At 2243 Shannon TACT officers M. Bibbs, J. Shelton, P. Long and F. Bartlett were all armed with 12 gauge pump shotguns. They would provide inner security for the east side and would be responsible for administering ordnance into the house prior to the actual entry. At 2237 Shannon covering the west side were R. Easley, J. Filsinger and P. Hale. All were carrying pump shotguns and would deploy ordnance from their side of the house.

These seven TACT officers situated on the east and west side of the house had their shotguns loaded with five ferret rounds of gas which they would all shoot into the house. After that the officers would each throw one artillery simulator and one can of C.S. (tear gas) into the house.

Covering the rear of the house, inside the vacant Curry address, were TACT officers York, McWilliams and Jones. Each armed with .223 bolt and scope rifles.

Dr. Milnor, a police staff reserve, would be stationed near the house with an armed escort of TACT officers, and would move forward once Hester was brought out of the house. He would be assisted by fire department paramedics who sat a short distance away, on Boxwood, in their ambulance.

CHAPTER 26

Negotiations End

S ilence permeated the area like a covering of new snow that was occasionally interrupted by the howl of a north wind. Nothing moved on the block and nowhere near 2239 Shannon did any light penetrate the cloak of darkness.

Suddenly the innocent silence was broken by the urgency of police radio transmissions.

TACT 511: - **511 to all four units move into your positions.**
Dispatcher: - **511, to all four units, move into your positions, 511 to all four units move into your position at 0241 hours.**
Unknown TACT: - **67 call up at the command post.**
TACT 567: - **Okay, 67.**
Pugh: - **502 to 540, BE ALERT, OKAY, be alert. 569, 569.**
TACT 569: - **69.**
Pugh: - **Nobody can hear you.**
TACT 569: - **569, we are ready.**

The six officers walked out the northeast door from the school moving silently to the TACT command post at 2247 Shannon where officers checked each other's equipment once again. If someone had a problem with anything, it was better to find out before, the bullets started flying. It was almost time.

The back door of the house was slowly pushed open. The officers filed out, one at a time in single file, and began moving west through the back yard. The route had been scouted and cleared of anything that might cause undo noise or cause anyone of the group to trip.

The officers were lined up in reverse order. The officers who would use the ram, to batter the door, were up front, but would be the last in, after entry was made.

Those assigned to the inner perimeter, scanned the portion of the house within the area of their responsibility. Spotters and snipers on the roof of the school had the best view of the entire scene. It was reminiscent of being in the stands, watching the Memphis State Tigers play football. Only, no one on the roof felt much like yelling, nor did the drama unfolding in front of them, even remotely resemble a sporting event.

Music: - **500 to 567 call the C.P.**
Hale: - **527.**
Dispatcher: - **527, go ahead.**
Hale: - **Was that call to C.P.?**
Dispatcher: - **567.**
TACT 567: - **Okay, 567**.

Uniformed officers were moved discreetly close to the classroom, where family members and friends of the suspects were being housed. The officers were not to let family members intervene or otherwise interfere in the pending operation. It was expected that pandemonium would break out once the assault began.

Additional officers had been moved to the outer perimeter to prevent anyone from rushing to the house. The outer perimeter stretched two full blocks in all directions. No one figured there would be much trouble from anyone in the neighborhood, but those in charge were not going to take that chance.

TACT 513: - **567, when you are ready just say, ready.**
Dispatcher: - **513 to 567 when you are ready say, ready.**
TACT 567: - **567 how do you read.**
Dispatcher: - **All clear to 567.**
TACT 567: - **I read the information, it has been taken care of.**

Flashlights had been fastened to the barrels of the M-16 assault rifles carried by Rutherford, Watson and Summers. McNair, who had devised the plan to be used, was armed with a short barrel, Remington, 12 gauge pump shotgun.

They attached flashlights to the barrels, to free up their hands. The light would be used to illuminate the house and help in quickly identifying friend or foe. Where ever the gun was pointed the light would follow, and the sudden beam would be directed into the face of anyone encountered by the unit, having the dual purpose of disorienting anyone TACT members met, and allowing rapid and accurate identification.

Several problems could not be overcome. The uncertainty of the layout of the house, the true number of occupants and the number and type of weapons and amount of ammunition for the weapons was still not known.

TACT 527: - **527 to 513 we are ready.**
TACT 513: - **513 stand by.**
TACT 513: - **541 stand by.**
TACT 541: - **541, did you advise us to stand by?**

TACT 513: - **Check 541.**
TACT 513: - **513, we got the time, 541.**

The more intelligence that had been gathered the more muddled the situation became. Because of this lack of hard information, all persons encountered other than Hester would be treated as an armed suspect. The team moved out through the rear of 2247 Shannon, walked behind 2243 Shannon and crept up to the south door of the target house. McNair checked with Huff to insure team two was ready.

TACT 541: - **Check 541.**
Unknown TACT: - **Negative 541.**
Dispatcher: - **513 to 541.**
TACT 513: - **13 to 541.**
Unknown Car: - **270 to 53.**

Music: - **500 go ahead.**
Unknown Car: - **70 to 500, secure at this time.**
Music: - **Okay 500. 500 TO ALL UNITS, 500 TO ALL UNITS, Signal Q, Signal Q, 500 the situation secure.**

McWilliams, from his vantage point inside the Curry address, watched as the ghostly shapes lined up at the back door. Once the primary assault team had gotten to the back door, he could provide little in the way of help. Anything that happened would have to be dealt with by the team. He would not risk a shot with so many officers, so close to the house.

Slowly, McWilliams scanned the windows, on the rear of the house, looking for any movement, through the scope of his rifle. If movement, of any kind, was detected, he would shout out a warning over his radio. His blood shot eyes saw nothing amiss and no words of warning would be needed from his parched throat.

Further down Shannon Street, a fire department pumper was readied, in case any of the ordinance shot off during entry, started a structure fire.

The snipers and spotters, perched on top of the school and within the houses on either side of the target house, watched intently for any movement or sounds, from within the house. This was the critical moment. This was one of the most vulnerable phases of the entry. The team was at the back door, surprise their best ally. The door had to be hit and entry made, before the occupants knew what hit them.

If the entry team took fire, before the breach was accomplished, they might suffer losses and never make it inside. All it would take for things to turn to shit would be someone in the house to glance out the back window and see the heavily armed men at the back door.

The secondary team had taken up their positions around the front and sides of the house. TACT officers, armed with shotguns, loaded with blue cased shotgun shells, waited for the order to dispense gas. Some officers were sweating in the thirty degree weather. Over one hundred pairs of eyes watched the tiny white house. One hundred pairs of ears waited for the sounds of the explosions. The seconds dragged by, as an eerie silence, washed over the scene.

In the distance, the barely audible thump-thump sound, of the police helicopter could be heard, as it circled in a holding pattern.

The TACT officer on the school roof looked down, his heart kicking into a higher gear, but his thoughts were slower, sadder and finally filled with a cautious shred of hope. *We're coming to get you Bobby. Sorry, it took so long son, but the cavalry is on its way.*

Dispatcher: - **500 to all units, 500 to all units, signal Q, TEAM LEADERS THE SITUATION IS YOURS.**
TACT 541: - **541, ready.**
Unknown TACT: - **541, I am with you if you are ready.**
Unknown TACT: - **Correct on that information.**
TACT 513: - **ALL UNITS BEGIN SIGNAL THREE, SIGNAL THREE.**

Dispatcher: - **513 to all units signal blue, 513 to all units signal blue.**

The night began to fill with the sound of breaking glass and the hiss of escaping gas.

CHAPTER 27
Dynamic Entry

January 13th, 1983
3:04am

S hotgunned ferret rounds blasted through panes of glass striking walls and furniture, then bouncing erratically along the floors. As they hissed out thin wisps of grayish-white tear gas other officers ran along the outside, flinging hand held canisters of still more tear gas through shattered windows. In seconds, thick clouds were billowing through the house.

The effect of the gas was instant on everyone inside, invading noses, mouths and eyes. Vision blurred, burned, eyes clamped shut. Throats felt scorched. Oxygen-deprived lungs sent panicked messages to brains.

Tear gas canisters tumbled across floors and furniture, a couch in the living room began to smoke and smolder as it ignited from a canister that struck and tumbled across.

The six silent, black-clad, TACT officers were lined up single file as they crouched by the back door. The lead man held one side of a red, four foot piece of steel. A double pat on the center of his back told him it was time. He and the second man in formation stood up, clutching steel welded handles on either side of the ram, as they moved to door. The remaining four men moved as one. The seventy-five pounds of vests, bullets and cold steel each man was burdened with was ignored as they lined up just to the right of the door. One of the four slid his hand along the top of his M-16. A gentle tug of the gray duct taped flashlight told him it was still snugly

secured to the barrel of his rifle.

The moonlit shadows cast by bulky equipment and bug-eyed gas masks projected images of fearsome, hellish creatures.

The sounds of shattering glass continued to fill the air as flash bangs and artillery simulators were tossed through windows. The deafening explosions shook the house rattling furniture, teeth and bones, each one splitting the darkness with a searing flash of light.

Ray and Hubbard swung the ram back and then forward crashing it against the back door. Splinters of wood sprayed the masks of the officers as the door flew open. Ray and Hubbard jumped away from the door, hugging the outside wall.

Watson leapt through the door first, firing off a pre-planned three round burst into the bar area of the smoke laden den. He was closely followed by Rutherford, Summers and McNair.

Muzzle flashes and the loud ragged echoes of pistol shots sounded from the kitchen. TACT officers immediately returned fire into the heavy smoke, smothering the pistol shots with the louder crisp, pop-pop-pop of their M-16 rifles.

There was no return fire as the four officers ran two at a time across the den into the kitchen, their positions in the meeting room doorway quickly covered now by Ray and Hubbard. Gunfire erupted again, this time, from the blackness of the southwest bedroom. TACT officers answered back with rifle and shotgun blasts at the shadowy figures that quickly disappeared from view.

Rutherford was hit in the back, the projectile slamming into the ballistic vest he wore. The impact sent him sprawling on to the kitchen floor.

Ill timed flash bangs continued to bombard the house and McNair signaled for a brief stop in the gas filled kitchen, waiting a few seconds for the gas and noise to subside enough to continue.

Rutherford rose to his knees, slapping a fresh thirty round magazine into his M-16. He heard pistol shots echoing from the smoky hallway and saw Summers and Watson crouched by the kitchen door firing at two men who had emerged from the gray smoke of the northwest bedroom door.

One of the men collapsed to the floor and the second man's body jerked violently before disappearing from sight.

Rutherford and McNair began inching their way into the hallway, towards the door of the bedroom where the men had just been. The beam from Rutherford's flashlight sliced through the smoke laden interior, passing over a bed and overturned table. Both officers caught a flash of movement. Rutherford fired a three round burst and McNair blasted a round from his shotgun.

Both officers crept towards the living room unaware if their shots had found their mark.

In the back of the house, Ray and Hubbard were silently moving through the den when gunfire from the southwest bedroom forced both officers to dive for the cover of the bar.

Gunshots thundered through the cold, dark house as Ray and Hubbard crept out from the bar and into the southwest bedroom. Both saw movement as they wheeled and fired at an armed man standing in the doorway that linked the southwest and northwest bedrooms. The man immediately dropped to the floor. Ray and Hubbard waited a minute, but saw no other movement in the northwest bedroom, and moved on, towards the living room.

The thin beams of light, swept from one side to the other of the disheveled, smoke-filled living room. Through the large lens of gas masks, six pairs of eyes scanned the floor. They saw his scuffed black leather shoes and torn uniform pants first. He was face down by the front door, the green carpet underneath him puddled and spattered with blood.

His hands were handcuffed behind his back, his rigid arms pulled to the right side, as if he was still trying to put his flesh torn hands up to defend himself. His leather jacket was bunched up above his waist.

Slowly they rolled Hester over.

His slender face was blackened, his dark curly hair matted with blood, his uniform shirt torn open, his bare white stomach and chest ghostly pale in the thin beams of light. His eyes were open.

Through the swirl of smoke they stared down at the face as it stared blankly back.

Sadness filled them all, a guilt filled sadness from a promise not kept.

They slowly lifted the body and moved it gently away from the door and then laid it back down. The front door was cracked open. A choked voice hollered out to the officers in the yard that they were bringing Bobby out.

Watson and Summers slung their rifles over their shoulders before picking Hester up and carrying him across the porch. They placed him on the frosted sidewalk, face down under the covering of the giant oak, his head near the front porch. Others stood guard in the living room, their rifles trained on the unsecured rear of the dark and now quiet house.

A voice came over the radio, tight and quick in its tone.

TACT 567: - **67 send the doctor on down. 567 send a doctor down.**
Dispatcher: - **Okay, 567.**
Maxey: - **503, have the ambulance pull down in front of the C.P.**

Reserve police officer Dr. Milnor and two TACT officers moved from cover and dashed across the yard to Hester.

Maxey: - **503, we need a stretcher put out in front of the school with the ambulance.**

Milnor knelt down to check for a pulse, but felt none. Hester's body was already stiff with the signs rigor mortis.

He pronounced Robert Hester dead at 3:13am.

From the roof of the school, an officer called out and asked about Hester. A TACT officer looked up at the roof, and slowly extended his arm, gesturing with his thumb in a downward motion.

Dr. Milnor was told to get back to cover. TACT officer Ray stepped out of the house holding his bloody hand, badly injured on his entry through the rear door. When McNair saw it, he gestured towards an ambulance. An officer ran up and helped Ray away from the yard.

Music: - **500 to those on security move up, those on security move up.**
Pugh: - **502 to 500 we are not secure in the building here, we are not secure in the house.**

McNair signaled to the assault team that a second sweep of the house was to begin. As his team moved through again, McNair began to worry about trying to secure the maze like house with one team.

Watson and Summers crept down the hall and into the smoke filled kitchen as they worked their way through the den. They entered the southwest bedroom and crept to the same connecting door where Ray and Hubbard had shot a man earlier. Rutherford, McNair and Hubbard edged their way down the black hall to the east door of the same bedroom.

Both teams saw a man holding a pistol crawling across the lifeless bodies on the floor. Quick bursts of M-16 fire struck him and he lurched forward, unmoving.

Watson slipped into the den as Summers began checking the southwest bedroom. He saw a flicker of movement at the far end of the bed and signaled to McNair to back him up. Summers stepped up on the mattress and looked over the edge of the bed, the butt of his M-16 pulled back into his shoulder. On the floor, he saw a man lying on his back clutching a pistol. Summers fired a three round burst into his head, then reached down, and wrenched the gun from his hand. He laid the cocked pistol on the bed.

McNair's patience with the odd, circular configuration of the house and shortage of personnel had finally reached its end. He moved back to the front door and yelled for additional TACT officers to assist with securing the house.

Quinn: - **501, have the second assault move in front of the house.** Hale: - **527 to 501 we are being used here in the house at this time.**

A second team of TACT officers, Bland, Bugg, Filsinger, Hale, Long and Shelton moved into the house. The second team was given specific rooms to secure and watch until the sweep was completed.

The primary assault team then conducted a third sweep of the house to look for other hiding places and basement or attic accesses to the house.

Music: - **To the officers in the house in the rear of the assaulted house, we need you to report to the command post right away.**
Unknown TACT: - **569, we are in route, will clean our equipment.**
Maxey: - **503, advise 1010**(Director Holt), **we are going to check and see if there is an attic, the house is not secure at this time.**
Dispatcher: - **503, 1010.**
Holt: - **Check.**
Dispatcher: - **1010, 503 advises they are going to let some of the gas clear and then check the attic, see if there is an attic, the house is not secure at 0338 hours.**

A third sweep of the house turned up no further suspects.

At 3:42am McNair ordered all TACT officers out of the house. The house had been secured.

Outside, patrol officers hugged and cried. They gathered in small groups on the street, whispering quietly, as they stared at Hester's body on the lawn. Television cameras lit up the area as smoke floated out of the house and into the cold morning air.

The TACT officers slowly walked out of the house and across the yard, their heads down, and their weapons to their side. None spoke, their emotions held in check for now, as they slowly made their way to their command post. The large white cobra shoulder patches on their sleeves shone brightly against their black uniforms as each member disappeared from sight behind 2243 Shannon.

Quinn: - **Have security meet us at the scene.**
Dispatcher: - **501, Security Squad meet them on the scene.**
Unknown TACT: - **Information to all TACT units the assault has been turned over to the Security Squad, report to the Command Post.**

The officer on the roof looked down into the front yard at Hester's body lying in the yard. There was an odd light playing off it, making it difficult to discern whether it was truly a body or discarded debris from the house. The officer wondered why Hester was still lying there. Investigators were just standing around Bobby looking at him.

Why don't they cover him up?

Why hadn't they picked him up and put him in an ambulance, *Jesus Christ*, how long are they gonna leave him there? The officer knew the answer to his own question but emotion had clouded his police training.

The officer slowly pushed himself to his feet, and spat on the roof. As he slung the strap of his rifle across his shoulder, he looked back one more time at the little white house and the lonely dark silhouette of Bobby lying crumpled under the out stretched limbs of the great oak. He turned and slowly walked away, his post now relinquished.

CHAPTER 28
Hester Taken Away

A t 2:45am, nineteen minutes before the assault began, Director Holt walked into class room 138. The room housed the press corp, including national and mid-south news agencies, along with reporters from local television and two Memphis newspapers. It had been inside this room that a nickname was created for the suspects inside the house: The Shannon Street Seven.

Holt told the media that he wasn't there to give a statement but to let them know he had given the order to send in the TACT unit.

"We've made the decision. We've got to go. Wish us luck,"

A similar scene happened with the families when an officer came to a classroom where they waited, and told them that police would be assaulting the house in a few minutes.

As the first explosions from artillery simulators reverberated through the school, family members screamed out. Some tried to run to the white house at 2239 Shannon, while others tried climbing through the school windows. Officers struggled to keep everyone under control.

The sound of tear gas being shot into the house, mingled with the noise of flash bangs and bursts of gunfire brought panic and hysteria. In seconds, the halls of the elementary school were filled with the tearful wailing of relatives, wives and mothers. Dorothy Sanders screamed they were going to kill her son.

Another female began cursing police officers who would not let her leave the school, threatening to *'kill all of the mother fucking officers'*.

Off duty officers, assigned to a room near the families, were called in to assist on-duty officers in restraining some of the grief stricken family members.

After the all clear signal was given by the TACT unit, the same officer who told the families of the impending assault walked back to the class room and made a solemn announcement to the families: *They're all gone.*

Slowly, the people in the school moved outside into the darkness. As they made their way slowly to the police barricades, their faces turned grim.

Police walked the street with tears in their eyes. Mayor Hackett, who had been present all but one hour of the incident, stood underneath the front awning of the school, arms folded, as he stared unblinking, towards the house.

City council members J. O. Patterson Jr, Billy Hyman, Pat Vander Schaaf, Jeff Sanford, Michael Hooks, James Ford and Oscar Edmonds were also in the group of on lookers at or near the school.

Six miles away from Shannon Street, at Methodist Central hospital, a police officer made a long walk down a empty hall towards the small room where Anita Hester awaited news of her husband. When he got to the door of the small room, he paused for a moment to compose himself. After another minute, he went inside.

Approximately 4:00am

In the quiet darkness of the early morning, an orange and white ambulance pulled up slowly and parked in front of the white house. Two men got out and walked to the back doors.

They opened the doors and pulled a stretcher out of the back. They slowly wheeled it into the yard, across the grass, stopping next to Bobby Hester's body.

TACT officer Rutherford and another officer picked Hester up as gently as they could, and laid him on the stretcher. A white sheet was carefully unfolded and placed over his still form. The medics then wheeled the covered stretcher to the ambulance, where they lifted and slid it inside. The doors closed with a soft thud.

One of the men pulled a piece of paper from his shirt pocket and began speaking with a group of men standing near the ambulance. The driver wrote something down, and after a few seconds, he folded up the paper and got into the ambulance. It moved slowly down the street, followed by an unmarked police car with a single investigator inside.

Fifteen minutes later, the ambulance turned into the parking lot of City of Memphis Hospital. The driver swung in a semi-circle and backed towards the door of the brown brick building. After stopping, both men got out, opened the back doors and pulled the stretcher out, and eased it on to the black pavement. They wheeled it down the battleship gray ramp to the sliding door. One of the men pushed the large red button next to the door. Several seconds later, a man in a lab coat opened the door and the stretcher was taken inside.

The medics guided it through the small, single windowed viewing room and through another set of faded white metal doors.

The stretcher was rolled onto a large stainless steel floor scale. The weight of the stretcher and its passenger was noted. The stretcher was then wheeled through yet another door, into a large white room, with a concrete floor and a large drain in the center. Above the drain was a stainless steel table, and above that, a cluster of six large silver hooded lights. The stretcher was rolled up to the table and the body was lifted from it and on to the bare, cold table.

Neither man took notice of the overwhelming odor that emulated from the room. There had been a time when both men could smell the odor before even stepping through the sliding door. After successive trips over the years into these rooms, the smell was no longer even an afterthought.

The two men wheeled the empty stretcher out of the room and again placed it on the scale. The weight was noted a second time. The driver pulled his sheet of paper out and began speaking with a man at the desk, near the scale.

Sgt. Landers stood with them. With bloodshot eyes, he scribbled down information, while at the same time, providing details and facts to the white-coated man at the desk. The driver and his partner wheeled their stretcher out.

Landers took a deep breath as he walked into the room, stopping not far from the table. In his hand was a Polaroid camera. He lifted it to his eye and began taking pictures. With each flash and whirl of the camera, picture after picture of the body came out.

Other people were in the room. They wore light blue surgical gowns and gloves, and were talking softly, taking their own notes, and waiting. After a while, one of the medical personal began filling out the Report of Investigation by County Medical Examiner.

The body lying on the table was designated A83-30 / C83-158. The first set of numbers was the Autopsy number and the second set was the case number. Each line was filled in and appropriate check boxes marked.

Decedent: R.S. Hester. Race: W. Sex: M. Age: 34.

Under type of death, the check box for violent was marked with an **X**. Under the check boxes, in the comment section, the word beating, was written in cursive. Date: 1-13-83. Time: 0355.

On the bottom of the form, in the check box section, for manner of death, the box next to homicide was marked with an **X**.

Officers who had seen Hester's body when it was brought out of the house did not recognize him. Some said at the time that it was hard to discern if Hester was black or white. Within hours, rumors of Hester being burnt with cigarettes, his fingernails pulled off and even being castrated or mutilated began swirling about the police department.

In the Morgue, Landers completed taking Polaroid pictures of Hester. He laid the camera down and then took 35mm photographs.

In his notes, Landers described Hester as being fully clothed, wearing a black police leather jacket, one pair of blue uniform pants, and one blue uniform shirt, with badges and jewelry apparently torn from the left breast pocket. He noted the shirt had cuts to the cuff on the right sleeve. The uniformed pants had a snag or hole to the right leg, midway between the cuff and the knee. Landers used words like, *covered in* and *saturated*, to describe the different clothing and the amount of blood on each article.

Landers continued to make notations as Hester's outer clothing was removed.

Under the blue uniform, Hester was wearing a long, or insulated type underwear shirt, and long insulated type underwear pants. The underwear shirt had a hole in the right sleeve, in the elbow area. Hester was wearing one pair of white shorts, underwear, which were bloody to the buttocks area. Black socks, pair of black shoes.

Hester's left arm was under and across the bottom/back of his body going to the right side. His right arm was down to his side and right hand and wrist were next to the left wrist, indicating that his hands had been handcuffed behind his back.

The leather he was wearing was the two-belt type. One belt, the inner one, went through the loops of his trousers. The other was wider leather belt that covered the first. The two were fastened with Velcro.

The outer belt held the holster. It was empty. There was two cartridge, or extra rounds holders, on the belt. Each would normally contain six(6) rounds of ammunition. They were empty. There was a white handkerchief found in the pants pocket, still folded and apparently unused.

Prior to morgue personnel removing Officer Hester's clothing, they removed from his front pants pocket one set of keys with a whistle, a chrome pocket knife, and twenty-seven cents in change. In his rear pants pocket, a brown billfold was found. It contained his identification, driver's license, credit cards, and a ten dollar bill.

Pinned on the leather jacket was a Memphis Police Department badge, #480. It was the old type/style police badge that was sold to the officers when the new style badges were issued. There was a wedding ring on his left hand. The bruising and swelling to his knuckles prevented it from being removed.

Hester's clothing and personal items were placed separately in large brown paper sacks by Morgue Attendant Carl Jefferson, and given to Landers.

Landers checked Hester's body for injuries and made numerous photographs of his body after the uniform was removed. A body chart was prepared by Landers which noted all of Hester's visible injuries.

Officer Hester's head was bloody and swollen, with large, numerous lacerations to the top, back and side, and over the right eye. Hester's scalp appeared to be loose on the skull.

There were blue discolorations around the neck with an abrasion on the left collar bone.

The task of documenting the injuries continued as Landers moved around the table snapping photos and take notes. Words like *lacerations, bruising, bloody, broken* and *swollen* were used again and again to describe almost every part of Hester's body.

There was stiffness to the body joints where it appeared that rigor mortis had set in.

After 70 minutes, Landers walked out of the room and found a chair in a quiet hallway and collapsed into it. He closed his eyes, and squeezed the brown sack sitting on his lap.

After a moment, he let out a long sigh, opened his eyes and scribbled in his note pad that badge #480, one of the MPD I.D. pins, the set of keys, $10.27 in money, the brown billfold with the drivers license, credit cards and other personal items along with the folding pocket knife and a small daily calendar notebook, would be turned over to Mrs. Hester.

Lander's reasoned that they were personal property belonging to Hester and would not be needed for the investigation.

CHAPTER 29
Crime Scene Begins

January 13th, 1983

A s the last TACT officer cleared the yard, the investigative
chain of command kicked in.

The Violent Crimes Bureau was designated as the lead investigative unit, since Hester was the victim of a homicide. The Shoot Team/Security Squad was to assist. Lt. Wilson was to coordinate the overall investigation. He placed Sgt. Garner in charge of the Violent Crimes part of the investigation. Lt. Tusant designated Sgt. Hollie as the case investigator for the Security Squad investigation. Security Squad would directly investigate any officer who had discharged his or her firearm.

4:21am

Lt. Wilson stood in the middle of Shannon Street as he began issuing assignments to the investigators that were clustered around him.

Sgt. L. W. Hunt and F. J. Wheeler were told to begin a scene description of the outside of the house. Their job would be to meticulously record what they found and where it was located on the outside of the house. The investigators began taking notes on what they saw.

The scene description began in the middle of the street, looking southward, directly in front of 2239 Shannon.

The house is a one story, white, asbestos shingle...

Hunt and Wheeler began walking forward towards the house ignoring all other activity within the roped off crime scene.

The front porch is of two levels, the higher level being approximately a foot from the ground, is approximately 5 feet, running north and south and 10 to 12 feet, running east to west and appears to be of manmade broken tile...

They now stood near the porch.

Moving west across the porch, several spots of blood, which are heavily concentrated...

Sgt. J. M. King began the interior scene description. Sgt. F. R. Hester, of the Criminal Intelligence Bureau, who was not related to Bobby, videotaped the interior of the house before anything was moved.

Sgt. Hollie and Officer D. W. Cooper of Security Squad were told to assist in maintaining the integrity of the outside scene by monitoring who came and went. Some officers said privately that Security Squad was only there to spy on the police and note any irregularities or misconduct during the scene investigation.

Sgts. Wheeler, Collier and Hammers went to the Security Squad Office to interview the members of the TACT unit's primary assault team.

The interviews were routine anytime an officer fired a weapon whether on or off duty. The Security Squad had to conduct an investigation to determine if the shooting was justified or not. It made no difference whether anyone was struck by the gunfire or not.

In this case seven suspects were dead as a result of police gunfire. Seven counts of homicide that had to be investigated by Security Squad.

At the conclusion of the investigation, they would present the case to the Attorney General's office of Shelby County who would decide if the homicides were justified or criminal. If justified, the six TACT officers would face no state criminal charges. If criminal, then those TACT officers deemed to be culpable would be prosecuted.

3:55am

Lt. Wilson sent cars to bring Dr. J. S. Bell, Dr. C. W. Harlan and Dr. O. C. Smith of the Shelby County Medical Examiner's Office to the scene to examine the other seven bodies that remained inside.

4:38am

Dr. Harlan entered the residence with Lt. Wilson and Sgt. King. Harlan pronounced all seven dead at approximately 4:40am. He told Wilson and King that all seven appeared to have died within the last hour.

The doctors would also handle the forensic investigation. Over the next several hours, Harlan and the other doctors took numerous photographs and made an interior sketch of the house.

Approximately 5:00am

The Commander of the Crime Scene Squad, Captain C. Moore and Lt. B. Wright arrived on the scene. Portable lights from the Crime Scene vans were used to help illuminate both the inside and outside scenes.

Sgts. C. A. Russell, R. R. Clenney and Officer T. H. Harrison of Crime Scene began taking photos, processing the scene for prints, making sketches and collecting evidence.

8:15am

Ann Fowler and Paulette Sutton of the University of Tn. College for the Health Sciences Toxicology Department were brought to the scene by Sgt. P. Pyle.

Their job was to collect and evaluate bloodstains and other fluids at the scene and analyze for origin. In laymen's terms, Fowler and Sutton had to determine whose blood was where. Sutton, a Forensic serologist, had been working at U.T. for six years.

Outside the house, Hunt and Wheeler were still taking notes on the scene.

At the southeast corner of the house were five spent .38 caliber hulls and one live round (Aiken's). On the ground near the northeast corner of the house were five spent blue shotgun shells and a one dollar bill.

Their outside scene description, after being typed single spaced, would cover four pages.

While the outside scene was being processed, the blood bath on the inside of the house was being surveyed. The scene description from Sgt. King read like the final act of a horror movie.

A large pool of blood directly in front of the front door lying in that pool of blood was one broken watch, part of a metal name tag with the words Serving Since 1973, and the back clasp for the name tag. Also, near the puddle of blood lay a second clasp and a M. P. D. collar emblem.

All the items had once been worn by Hester.

In front of the brick fire place, on the east wall of the living room, was a Kool filter king cigarette pack, which was empty and bloody. Near the cigarette pack was an eight inch leather slap also covered in blood. Pieces of broken mirrors lay strewn on the floor. The mirrors had once rested above the fireplace.

On the mantel above the fireplace was a picture of Lindberg and his wife. On either side of the picture were two decorative wine bottles. The three items stood unscathed through thirty hours of flying bullets and tear gas canisters.

Above the mantel, arranged three high and five wide in a pattern were fifteen mirror tiles. Blood spray covered them. Lying on the suspended coffee table was a four cell, police type, kel-light, which was covered in blood. A rifle scope, with blood stains, and a Memphis Police Department badge, with the number 480 on it. There was a blood stained fingerprint etched on its silver surface.

The badge had been worn by Hester.

Discarded on the floor was a police radio # 33, face down, with no battery. Near the radio was another chandelier prism, a blue Bic lighter and another police type kel-light.

While investigators, forensic experts and crime scene personnel swarmed over the scene, the crowds watching continued to grow.

Onlookers, friends, and neighbors stood behind police lines two blocks away and stood silently, watching the non-stop activity swirling around 2239 Shannon.

Many complained that only white policemen were investigating the scene and the black officers were being used to direct traffic and for crowd control.

Betty Allen, a neighbor, told reporters that she thought it was low down of the police.

Lavallis Webster, another neighbor, said that all Sanders ever did was read the Bible every day and have Bible study at his house. Her opinion was that the police could have gotten the seven suspects out alive.

Mose Carter, whose brother was David Jordan, was trying to find out if David was one of the dead. Carter lamented, that if his brother was dead, it was the will of God. Jordan had told Mose, during one of their discussions, that it was his job to put the word out that the world was coming to an end.

Another local resident, Charles Bright, had an opinion that was more of a question. "I don't really think it was necessary for them to kill all the people, because maybe they was held hostage themselves. Could've been some lives taken that shouldn't been taken."

Some in the crowd talked of Sanders' ill feelings and outward hatred for white people and police officers. These same people then said that the police were not justified in killing the suspects.

There were no recorded comments from anyone in the crowd who spoke of officer Hester and who should be held accountable for his death.

As one of the investigators walked through the scene, he wondered if Lindberg Sanders had gotten his wish. The little house that his wife and he had done so much work on was now a crime scene. Rooms that had once been decorated with pictures were now riddled with bullet holes and smeared with blood. The place that had once smelled of flowers now smelled of tear gas and death.

Sanders had foretold the end of the world. An end that included death and bloodshed. It seemed he had got his wish.

Investigators, taking notes and snapping pictures, recorded all that they had seen in the house. But of the thousands of words and images recorded by investigators, there came a single item that at least in the minds of the investigators, seemed to say it all.

On the floor, near a tear gas canister and a blood-soaked coffee cup was a pile of cassette tapes. One title stood out, for all to read: "Be a Happy Man".

CHAPTER 30
Tact Interviews Begin

January 13th, 1983
5:00am

The eleven men sat in the hallway smelling of tear gas and cordite. They stared blankly from blood shot eyes, some with blood stains on their sweat soaked uniforms. All were still hyped up with adrenaline pumping through bodies, but at the same time, beaten down by cold that had eaten at them for over thirty hours. Their faces showed nothing.

They were facing the first of many hours of interviews on what their actions had been prior to and during the assault. The officers knew what was coming but that didn't make it any easier on their weary minds and fatigued bodies.

Seven black men, who had participated in the murder of a white police officer, were dead. Only two guns and a box cutter knife had been found in the house.

The public was already demanding answers.

It was time to get some.

(In the following statements some questions and answers were removed for brevity. What is reprinted is the actual text from the statements).

Jonny Filsinger was the first to begin as he sat in front of Sgt. Wheeler in an interview room in the Security Squad office with a tape recorder running.

Q: For the record state your name?
A: Jonny Filsinger.
Q: Jonny are you aware this statement is being recorded.
A: Yes sir.
Q: State in detail everything that you did when the house was assaulted by the TACT unit at 2239 Shannon?
A: What we did was to put gas into the house, that was my job, to shoot five ferret rounds into the house, two gas grenades, and also a simulator. At that point I was to take cover until we were needed to secure the interior of the house.
Q: What position were you at?
A: I was on the northwest corner of the perpetrators house.
Q: From the position that you had taken outside the house, did you ever see anyone brought outside the house?
A: Yes sir, I did. They brought the patrolman out, Hester. Two TACT officers drug him outside to below the steps on the walkway and then they went back inside.

Q: For the record state your name?
A: Sgt. **J. D. Bland**.
Q: What part did you take in the assault on the house?
A: My team was assigned as back-up for the primary assault team when they made the initial assault to provide security inside the house, held the rooms as they made their sweep through it.

Q: Prior to you entering the house did you see anyone brought out of the house?
A: Yes.
Q: Who did you see brought out of the house?

A: I saw a body brought out and laid in front of the house. It appeared to be a police officer. He was handcuffed with his hands behind him and he was immobile. At that time he appeared to be deceased.

Q: Could you tell if he had any injuries to him?

A: Could see blood all about his head. Didn't have time to take a closer look...bloody all about his head.

Q: **Patrolman Bugg**, how long have you been employed by the Memphis Police Department?

A: Thirteen years.

Q: What was your assignment in regards to 2239 Shannon?

A: I was positioned in the rear of the house, just west of 2239 Shannon. It was my job to cover Cockrell and Easley when they put tear gas into the house. After they put tear gas in the house they ran down by the steps and waited until the operation was over. After the operation was over, officer K. McNair said he needed one man with a gas mask on to help secure the inside of the house and went into the house and directed me to the rear of the house where he told me to secure, which I did.

Q: For the record state your name?

A: **Robert J. Shelton.**

Q: State in detail everything that you did during the assault of the house.

A: I was assigned three men. Our assignment as secondary or back-up assault team was to lay down non-lethal weaponry such as tear gas and artillery simulators into the house as a diversion while the primary assault team went through the door on the initial assault in an attempt to get the officer out of the house and complete the mission. We took up the position, I myself took up the position behind a black Ford van which is located in the driveway just east of the perpetrator's house and I was laying down cover, security cover, for my three officers or team leaders who were putting the tear gas into the hose. At the time the signal blue was given, signal blue means gas for the TACT unit people. My three team leaders, patrolman Pat Long, patrolman Eddie Bartlett and patrolman M.E. Bibbs started throwing gas and artillery simulators into the windows of the house as a diversionary tactic while the primary assault team went through the rear door located on the south side of the perpetrators house...

Q: Could you tell what injuries, if any the body that you saw lying on the sidewalk in front of the house that you presume was officer Hester, had sustained?

A: At first, when I looked I was unsure whether it was a male, black or a male, white because the head of this body was almost black. Then when I looked at the hands being handcuffed behind his back, his hands were white or I could tell that it was a male white. With the intelligence gathering data that we had I knew that patrolman Hester was the only male white inside, was suppose to be the only male white inside the house.

Q: For the record state your name?

A: **Patrick Elvin Long.**

Q: What was your assignment during the assault?

A: My assignment was to supple tear gas and sound blast devices into the northeast side of the house while the TACT team was getting ready to make entry.

Q: State in detail everything that occurred during the assault of the house?

A: As we were given the signal to proceed, set up on the house at that particular location, mine was the northeast side of the house, should say northeast window, I waited at that position until a signal blue was given to shoot five ferret rounds through the window followed by a large gas grenade and a sound blast device which I did right prior to the entry by the attack team.

After I finished that I did take cover behind a car which was in the driveway on the east side of the house and waited until the TACT team secured the house.

Q: How many shots could you determine that came from the inside of the house?

A: It was a large amount, probably between fifty and seventy-five.

Q: **Officer Hale**, how long have you been employed with the Memphis Police Department?

A: It will be fifteen years in March.

Q: Explain what your duties were at this particular situation and what you observed and what actions you took during this period of time?

A: Our duties on this particular night was we were going to put in the gas for the assault team prior to their entry into the house. I fired five rounds of the shotgun through, threw in one canister of gas and one sound flash grenade. After I put this ordinance in I took position back from away the house in a prone position...

The interviews with the TACT officers stationed outside the house were not considered as vital to the investigation as the ones that would be taken from the primary assault team. It was this team that had received hostile fire and it was their weapons that had silenced that fire. It would be the primary assault team that would be asked the tougher questions and would have to provide the answers.

CHAPTER 31
A-1

As each TACT officer took his turn answering questions at the old police headquarters building the investigation on Shannon continued.

A police issued radio, stamped with # 41 - M P D - North Precinct, lay on the floor covered in blood.

Blood spattering and thickening bloody pools were found on the living room floor, walls, the inside of the door, on the left door facing, and a beige love seat. The carpet underneath the love seat, the black leather police jacket lying on the couch and the back of Hester's wristwatch found on the floor were described by investigators as being coated in blood.

The ivory colored curtains on the front window, above the love seat, were partially burnt. Two chandelier prisms found on the floor, near the front windows, were blood drenched. A couch and round chair were heavily stained with blood.

In the northeast bedroom investigators found a silver ink pen, a small note pad and a broken radio antenna lying scattered on the floor.

There were two rooms that had not yet been sketched. Two bedrooms that investigators had not conducted scene descriptions on were ones containing the bodies of the suspects.

One was the northwest bedroom. In it was a small table, chair and a broken mirror lay atop the bed. On the green carpet were six bodies sprawled on the floor, side by side. All six bloody suspects lay in a single line between the two bedroom doors that led from the room.

In the southwest bedroom one body lay on the floor in a pool of blood.

Because the bodies could not be identified at the time, Dr. Harlan numbered each body. The numbering began with the body on the southern most side of the northwest bedroom and ended with the body in the southwest bedroom.

A-1- Northwest bedroom- male, black, resting against the south wall partition, on his back, feet towards the east wall partition and his head extended to the west. Clad in blue jeans, an orange and blue insulated jacket, beige undershirt and brown socks. He was clutching a silver box opener razor in his left hand.

B-2 - Northwest bedroom - male, black, head was extended east and his feet were extended west. Clad in a blue jacket, white shirt, blue jeans, brown belt and tennis shoes.

C-3 - Northwest bedroom - male, black, head was extended west, feet extended east, Clad in a black jacket, blue jeans, brown crepe sole shoes. Underneath this body was a blue steel .38 caliber, S&W, model 10, six shot revolver with over sized wood grips, serial number D470679. Weapon was bloody and contained three rounds and three empty chambers.

(*This was the pistol issued to Officer Hester.*)

D-4 - Northwest Bedroom - male, black, head extended east and feet extended west. Clad in a brown jacket, blue jeans, blue shirt and black tennis shoes with white soles.

E-5 - Northwest bedroom - male, black, head was extended west and his feet extended east. Clad in black jeans, gray, orange and white sweater, large blue belt and blue socks.

F-6 - Northwest bedroom - male, black, head was extended east and feet extended west. Body wrapped in a brown sleeping bag or bed comforter.

A-1 through F-6 were lying between the south and east door of the northwest bedroom, side by side, with their bodies touching.

G-7 - Southwest bedroom - male, black, lying on his back, head extended west and feet extended east between round bed and south wall. Clad in white and blue socks, blue jeans, brown shirt with red writing and a white jersey type jacket. A one by six board that was four feet long was lying on top of his chest.

A blue steel, 38 caliber, S&W, model 10, six shot revolver, with over sized wood grips, serial number D647991, was found on the edge of the bed. The hammer was cocked and contained two 38 caliber rounds and four empty chambers.

(*This was the pistol issued to Ray Schwill.*)

7:19am

Four medic ambulances were lined up on Shannon in front of the house with their back doors open. The seven bodies were brought out and loaded up before being transported to the City Morgue.

Once the bodies had been removed investigators Garner and Hunt conducted a search and wrote a scene description for the northwest bedroom.

Several spent .38 caliber hulls, a spent .223 caliber hull, and a bloody pair of white tennis shoes was recovered. The T.V. was lying face down and had been partially lying on two of the suspects. A large, dried blood stain was in front of the south door. An FM stereo, Walkman type, Lloyds brand radio was lying by body F-6.

The southwest bedroom contained a large round canopy type-bed stained in blood.

In the sunken den, a two foot tall glass marijuana pipe and ten other marijuana pipes of various sizes.

Blood spattering covered the hall way leading off the living room.

And so it went the methodical process of noting, marking, photographing, sketching, measuring, everything and anything. Nothing could be left out because the physical crime scene would tell a story that no human had lived to tell.

Investigators knew that what they did here would serve as pieces of a bloody puzzle that hopefully could tell that story. They realized, too, that some pieces might not be found.

Lt. Wilson instructed Sgt. Garner to determine the total number of shots fired both inside and outside the house.

Garner came up with eighty holes on the inside and outside of the house. Garner's estimate was not exact, as one bullet, could have caused multiple holes. It was also difficult to determine if some holes were caused by bullets fired from inside or outside the house.

Crime Scene would issue a multi-page report on the total number of live and spent cartridge cases, spent bullets and bullet fragments that were recovered from inside and outside the house.

Forty spent .223 casings were found inside the house and ten on the outside. One live cartridge was found outside. Four spent shotgun shells were recovered inside the house and twenty two were found outside.

Twelve spent .38 caliber casings were found inside and five outside. Nine live .38 cartridges were found inside the house and seven outside the house. Four spent rounds were found inside but the caliber could not be determined. Two bullet fragments were found in and three outside. One spent double-00 buckshot pellet was found inside.

Thirty four separate entries were made as the crime scene personnel located, photographed and measured each find. They began from the outside, at the southeast corner of the house, through the back door, and into the house.

Around noon, on January 13th, Sgts. Collier and Hollie met with Lt. Wilson and two investigators from the Shelby County Attorney General's Office in front of 2239 Shannon.

Wilson briefed the two investigators as to the crime scene, evidence collected and the positioning of the bodies. Wilson then briefed Collier and Hollie before instructing them to provide assistance to Ann Fowler and Paulette Sutton who were taking blood samples from the house.

Lt. Wilson told Sgt. Hollie to obtain carpet samples from the areas of the house where the bodies had been found in order to determine if any shots went through the carpet and into the floor. It was near 3:00pm on when Fowler and Sutton finally finished their work at the scene.

Sgt. Harrell, from Crime Scene, processed the items located on the living room coffee table for prints before taking them to 201 Poplar to be tagged in the property room.

Sgt. Hollie and Collier removed carpet and checked the floor underneath. They could not locate any bullets or holes caused by bullets. The bloody carpet pulled from the floor was tagged at the property room.

At 3:40pm, on January 13, just over twelve hours after the TACT assault on the house, Sgt.Hollie relinquished custody of the house over to Arrilia Pollion. Ms. Pollion was Lindberg Sanders' sister.

On a piece of paper were the handwritten words, *House at 2239 Shannon to Ms. Pollion who is the sister of Lindberg Sanders.* Underneath Ms. Pollion put the date 1-13-83 and signed her name.

Hollie walked to his unmarked cruiser and with that the Memphis Police Department had completed their physical examination of the little white house.

CHAPTER 32
Tact Interviews End

January 13th
Security Squad Office
(In the following statements some questions and answers were removed for brevity. What is reprinted is the actual text from the statements).

K.K. McNair

Q: How long have you been with the TACT unit?

A: Seven years.

Q: On this particular night, what were your duties?

A: I was an assault team leader for the possible assault of the house.

Q: Okay, as an assault team leader, is there any instructions that you give your team? How do you handle that?

A: Well, we gather all the intelligence that's available and then we map out what we feel would be the safest and best way for us to handle the situation.

Q: How many times did you fire your weapon?

A: I fired my weapon twice.

Q: What type weapon were you firing?

A: An 870, Remington, pump shotgun.

Q: What was the lighting conditions in the house?

A: The lighting conditions were very poor.

Q: Do you know whether or not if you hit anyone with your shotgun?

A: No.

Q: You stated you found officer Hester in the front part of the house by the front door. What was his condition?

A: Officer Hester appeared to be dead. Was in fact dead.

Q: From your observation, could you tell what caused his death?

A: Sir, he was handcuffed with his hands behind his back and there was a tremendous amount of blood about his head. Other than that, I really don't know.

Q: Did you encounter anymore resistance?

A: Yes sir we did.

Q: What did you do then?

A: I personally didn't do anything. The men in front of me were the ones that encountered the resistance and took the appropriate actions.

Q: Before this assault, did you know for sure how many people were in the house?

A: We had been given intelligence that from time to time there was as few as four and possibly as many as seven or eight to nine in there.

Q: Okay, exactly how many were in the house?

A: There were seven male blacks and one male white officer.

Q: **Officer Rutherford**, I will ask you to state in your own words and in detail what your duties were in regards to this situation, what you observed and what actions you took during your assignment?

A: It was determined that we were to make entry into the house. I was to be the second officer to enter from the rear door on the south side of the building. Of course, I had my primary area of

responsibility upon entering the house. Tear gas and other pro-
visions were to be used prior to entering. A signal was given for
the use of tear gas and entry into the door on the south side of
the building. Directly upon making entry, we received from the
den, kitchen area. The assault was to be made by four initial officers and two back up officers. Upon receiving fire, returned fire
into this area. Tear gas and sound flash devices, artillery simulators were thrown into the house, for diversionary purposes and
to cover for us. We, like I said, returned fire to the area in which
we received fire. We then progressed into the area we received
fire, which was the den, kitchen area of the house. We didn't
locate anybody in that area. A few officers went into a hall area
right at the kitchen and to get into that area you have to pass
a hallway directly to your left. They passed through that hallway safely...correction, they passed in front of the hallway safely.
When my team relief passed through, I started in behind him.
Directly down the hall, one or two subjects appeared in a doorway down the hall and started shooting down the hall towards
us. They fired three or four shots I believe. I couldn't see, all I
could see mostly was muzzle blasts, it was very dark. A lot of tear
gas and a lot of smoke. I had a flashlight taped to the end of my
M-16. I put the light on them. I caught a glimpse of the subjects
hand. At that time I fired on the subjects, on which I ceased fire
and later on one or two of them was found dead. We continued
on in the direction we were going, into the central hallway and
into a bedroom that was directly off the kitchen. We swept down
the hall, myself and found Officer Bob Hester laying face down,
handcuffed, just by the front door. He was obviously dead. We
rolled him over and looked at him and at that point we hollered
we'd located the officer and we were going to take him out on
the front porch. We placed Officer Hester on the ground, sidewalk, just off the porch. Called for a doctor to come up and look
at him. The doctor ran up quickly and said he was dead and we

told the doctor to get back under cover. He went back. When we entered the house we went with full intent to only identify and be conscious enough to eliminate threats to ourselves. When we make an assault usually you do a search along the way. This was not done in this incident because we felt sure they were going to be ready to ambush us and what we needed to do was to locate them and isolate them. We knew there was the possibility to miss somebody.

Q: How many shots did you fire from your weapon?

A: During the confrontation or during the entire event?

Q: The whole incident?

A: Forty to forty-five rounds.

Q: Did you reload your weapon during this incident, if so, tell me approximately when and position where you had to re-load?

A: Yes, I did have to reload my weapon. I had a thirty round clip in my M-16. To be truthful, I'm not sure if I had to reload before the first confrontation or just after. I do remember reloading in the kitchen.

Q: Were you injured?

A: Something did hit me in the back and I had two vests on, I had a heavy vest on and a lighter vest on under it. Of course, I was knocked off my feet but as far as any injury, I don't believe so.

Q: For the record state your name?

A: **Robert O. Watson.**

Q: State in detail everything that occurred after you entered the rear door of the Shannon address?

A: Upon originally entering the rear door my plan was to fire initial fire into the bar area of the room upon entry and upon entry either simultaneously with my first shot or within the element of my first few shots I received direct fire..straight ahead from inside the house. As to how many shots, how many people were firing I don't know. I took cover to the bar and waited for the rest of the element to enter and we took position in the front room. We had a lapse in our time signals so the artillery simulators and bang flash devices being concluded prior to entry because they were going off with us in there. Upon securing that room and returning what fire we received I continued on into I think the den. I believe I fired, I felt like I took a round from an area straight away and I couldn't see where it was coming from and I saw a refrigerator door open and I saw a pair of shoes under the door which was later nothing but I fired one or two rounds into the refrigerator door. I felt like somebody was behind that door. There were points while moving in the house that received fire, returned fire and during those points I can't specifically say whether anyone was struck or not. When we did not receive fire, when I didn't receive fire, I didn't return fire. There was one room that I entered upon there was a male black laying among several other male blacks that was on his right side, had a gun either in his hand or near his hand. Upon seeing that I fired one or two shots and someone else, we entered the room at the same time, two doorways and they fired but I don't know who they were. That is the only incident inside the house that I can specifically say that I shot an individual, per se that I can identify.

Q: Do you know what room in this house this was?

A: I would assume it was one of the bedrooms because there were several individuals laying in there with him and they had already been shot and were of no threat. They were not fired on by me.

Q: Do you know how many people were shot inside the house?

A: I searched upon the conclusion of receiving fire, when I didn't hear any more firing or we weren't receiving any more firing or we weren't firing, we searched and I recall I think approximately five individuals that I saw prone and silent, head wounds. I didn't check them to make sure they were dead, I didn't shoot them further. They were no threat.

Q: Where did you find officer Hester?
A: I found him by the front door and this is on the original sweep and it may have still been some firing going on I don't remember, but I found Hester and when I initially saw him it was difficult to determine whether he was black or white.
Q: Who carried Hester out of the house?
A: Officer Summers and myself.

Q: Do you know who else fired their weapons inside the house?
A: I know other people did, but I can't specifically say I saw anybody fire. I assume that C.R. Summers fired. We were close together and we were confronted with fire in the doorway but I can't say that he fired. I mean upon being fired at you know,..I just tried to get my ass out of the house.
Q: Were you injured in any way during the assault on the house?
A: I broke a bridge, a tooth in half and I don't know how I did it. I have no idea but the bridge is broke in half.
Q: Did you immediately report to your supervisor that during the assault on the house that you had fired your weapon?
A: I didn't volunteer the information but I was confronted prior to being able to volunteer and I responded to yes.
Q: Is there anything else you would like to add to this statement?
A: I'd like to say that I am proud to have worked with those men in the house. I think they did a hell of a job.

Q: **Officer Summers**, how long have you been employed by the Memphis Police Department?
A: Thirteen and half years.
Q: What type weapon were you firing?
A: M-16.

Q: Do you know how many rounds you fired, how many rounds you fired from this weapon?

A: I think I fired approximately twenty rounds.

Q: Is this an automatic weapon?

A: Yes sir it is.

Q: After entering the house, in receiving fire, could you make out any type of person that was firing at you or could you just see the muzzle blast?

A: I really couldn't see anyone at that point. I was just in the two hallways providing covering fire for officer Watson, he's the one that was taking the rounds.

Q: To the best of your knowledge how many people in the house were fatally wounded by you?

A: One.

Q: Exactly where was officer Hester's body lying?

A: Uhh..right about, almost in front of the front door. Maybe just a little bit to the west, a couple feet to the west center. By the front door. I think we even had to move him forward just a little bit so we could get the door all the way open so we could get him out.

Q: In gathering the intelligence information regarding this situation, was there ever any mention of the owner of this house being somewhat of a gun-nut and possibly did have several different types of guns in the house?

A: Yes sir. We were advised three particular points in regards to the suspect that lived there. One that he may have had several different types of weapons in the house. Two that he is on drugs and had been held up in the house since Saturday taking some type of drugs with other people and the third thing we were advised was that he was some type of religious fanatic.

Q: After officer Hester was taken hostage, did you have an occasion to hear any type of conversation inside the house between the persons that were in it and officer Hester?

A: Yes sir. My duty as I arrived on the scene was to go to the house immediately west of the suspects location with officer Cockrell, where we stayed for the remainder time up to one hour prior to the assault. While we were there I did on numerous occasions hear officer Hester crying, begging for mercy. One time he begged them not to kill him. Very audible. Numerous cries for help, oh please God, Please God, no, things of that nature. This went on for quite some time. Somewhere around 3:30 in the morning officer Hester, you could tell he was receiving a tremendous beating. From the movement in the house, that they were in it seemed like there was two people at the same time administering this beating. Perhaps more but at least two. Then approximately around 3:30, the cries got so intent and it was obvious that the pain was so intent. It got to the point where the officer was extremely weak. His cries for help became very inaudible and then around 3:30 mark it became silent as far as crying from the officer and that was the last time I heard officer Hester's voice.

Q: **Patrolman Hubbard**, how long have you been employed by the Memphis Police Department?
A: Thirteen and a half years.
Q: Could you estimate how far you were from the subjects that you did fire at?
A: I'd say approximately ten feet.

Q: Officer Hubbard, at anytime while you were in the residence, were you confronted by the occupants, did any of them indicate to you that they wanted to surrender?
A: No, they did not.

January 16th, 1983
Sgt. Landers was east bound Walnut Grove as he crossed over I-240 South. He moved over to the right curve lane and turned into the parking lot of Baptist East Hospital. Landers walked through the lobby and got in the elevator.

Landers stepped out on the fourth floor and found his way to room 4146. He knocked on the door and walked in. The man he was going to interview was sitting up in bed, clad in navy blue pajamas. His right hand was heavily bandaged.

Q: Officer Hildre, state your name?
A: **Hildre A. Ray**.
Q: Officer Ray, how long did you remain at the location?
A: The entire time.
Q: The entire time?
A: From the time it started until approximately 3 o'clock Thursday morning when I went to the hospital.
Q: What was your duty or what was your number in the assault team?
A: I didn't have a number in the assault, I was the number five man. My duty was to use the battery ram on the back door to knock it down and to cover the backs of the other four officers who were in front.
Q: Did an officer assist you with the door?
A: Yes.
Q: Who was this officer?
A: Dave Hubbard.
Q: Officer Ray, what was you armed with?
A: I was armed with a 12 gauge shotgun.
Q: When you entered the house, how did you enter, describe the way in which you went?
A: When I entered the house we went into the big room on the south side of the house, I think they call it the prayer room. It looked like a den to me. I went directly in behind the other four officers, watching the bedroom. As they proceeded up into the kitchen, I went on up into the kitchen.
Q: What was your next action after you entered the kitchen from the den area on the landing?

A: After we got into the den area on the landing, we were still covering their backs and we started receiving fire down the hall which runs between two bedrooms.

Q: Is this going to be to the left?

A: It'll be to our left, back west.

Q: What did you do then?

A: At that time we, there is a bar on that corner. We laid behind the bar for a few minutes and then we started easing down the hall. We got down to the first bedroom and there was a closet immediately to our left. We took our flashlights and swept the bedroom and didn't see anything there. We tried to cover the door to the other bedroom at all times. After we checked the closet, we took a quick peep into the bedroom to our right and I observed a male black with what appeared to be a 38 caliber pistol, revolver.

Q: What actions did you take at this time?

A: I stood up and I fired one round out of the shotgun, looked back into the bedroom and the individual had fallen back to the north side of the bedroom maybe a foot and a half from where he was. We looked inside the bedroom and saw some more male blacks, but nobody was moving. We stood there maybe a minute and a half and no one moved. The other officers were going on up through this hall and so we went on up and started covering their backs.

Q: Did the officers you were covering, were you with them when they found Officer Hester.

A: No, I was still covering their backs. They found officer Hester and then I walked into the room where they found the officer.

Q: What happened then?

A: They carried officer Hester out. My hand was hurting. I got one of the officers, either Rutherford or McNair, to put his flashlight on my hand and told me to get the hell out of there, that I'd been hurt and whichever one of them it was. I'm not sure, McNair or Rutherford, took me by the arm and carried me to the front door and or carried me to a door, I believe it was the front and officer, some officer, it was a big officer, took me by the arm and carried me to the ambulance.

Q: How did you receive your injury to your hand?
A: I received it going through the back door. I got it caught between the handle on the bar we were using to knock down the door with the door.
Q: What was the extent of the injuries to the hand?
A: It busted my hand open in the palm. Broke my little finger.
Q: Officer Ray, describe how you fired the shotgun? I believe you mentioned, you, you're not, are you right hand or left hand?
A: Right hand.
Q: How did you fire the shotgun?
A: I had to fire the shotgun left handed.
Q: You advised he had a pistol you could see, do you know what position or where you would have struck the suspect?
A: I shot for his upper body. Either his chest or top part of his body.
Q: Approximately how far were you from the suspect?
A: Probably ten feet.
Q: Did you work the shotgun and inject a round at the door?
A: I did.
Q: In your initial sweep, when you went through the house, was every area searched at the time or what was the object of the first sweep?
A: The first sweep through the house was the sweep looking for officer Hester.

CHAPTER 33
Seven at the Morgue

January 13th, Approximately 9:00am
201 Poplar, 11th floor, Violent Crimes Office

S gt. Anderson picked up the phone at his desk and dialed the four digit number.

"Tunnel," the voice answered.

"Yea, I need to pick up a prisoner for a detective visit," Anderson said.

"The prisoner's name?" the voice asked?

"Thomas Smith," Anderson answered.

After giving the deputy jailer Smith's booking number, Anderson gave his desk number.

"We will call you back when he's ready," the jailer said.

Fifteen minutes later Anderson answered his phone.

"Smith's ready," the jailer said.

"Okay, send the elevator to eleven," Anderson said.

Anderson walked over to his small locker in the southeast corner of the office. He opened the locker, placed his pistol inside, and re-locked it. He then headed through the office into the lobby and across the hall to an elevator door.

He heard the whirl of the elevator as it approached the 11th floor. As the elevator door opened, the investigator Anderson had asked to go with him walked up and they both got on, standing silent for several seconds before the doors closed.

The elevator had no buttons that could be pushed. It was controlled by Shelby County jailers and when the elevator was sent to a certain floor, it would go to that floor and then come back to the underground jail wing known as the tunnel. The elevator could not stop on multiple floors on any one trip and in fact could only open on six floors within the building.

When the elevator doors opened, the two investigators walked out seven steps and stopped at the set of metal bars running across the hall from the ceiling to the floor. Anderson looked through the bars at the glass-enclosed control center. One of the jailers looked up, and seeing the two investigators, hit the door open button. The barred door slid open. Anderson and his partner walked another twenty steps before veering back to their left and around to the access door of the control center.

His partner signed his name in the detective's log as Anderson looked out through the security glass at the tunnels that all led away from the control center to other parts of the jail.

The two investigators walked out of the control center as Smith stepped out of tank one which was thirty feet away. Smith was led back to the elevator and all three men got on.

They rode in silence to the eleventh floor where the door opened and Smith was lead through the large office, with twenty paper laden desks, to the large interview room on the northeast side of the Violent Crimes office. Smith was placed in a chair and his leg was fastened to the chair with a leg iron.

9:35am

Thomas (T.C.) Smith sat in a chair across from Sgt. Anderson and C. Ritter. He had spent the last 11 hours in the jail, arrested after police suspected he and his wife, Charlene Smith had lied to them about T.C.'s involvement in the assaults on Hester and Schwill. At that time, he had been the only man to have been arrested in relation to the incident.

Anderson began reading...

The first paragraph contained Smith's personal information.

The second paragraph of the statement read: Thomas C. Smith, you are under arrest but have not been charged at this time in connection with the Criminal Homicide of Patrolman R.S. Hester. However, if our investigation deems it necessary you may be charged at a later date and time.

Anderson then read Smith his Miranda Rights.

Q: Do you understand each of the rights I have just explained to you?

A: Yes.

Q: Having these rights in mind, do you wish to make a statement at this time?

A: Yes.

Q: Do you know Lindberg Sanders?

A: Yes.

Q: Do you know where he lives?

A: He lives on Shannon.

Q: How long have you known him?

A: Since 1977, five years.

Q: Is he a leader of a religious group?

A: He was a teacher, well he was what everybody looked up to.

Q: Did he have worship services of a religious nature at his home?
A: Yes.
Q: Basically describe his religious teachings or thoughts?
A: One thing that he taught all of us was to follow instructions, what you read in the Bible and don't call it a lie. For the last month, teachings were just for the men. They left their wives at home. Sometimes the wives would come. I read in there where meat offerings were made but we don't do that. He was the elder. What was happened was we was supposed to have been revived and we had been meeting this month more than we had in a long time. He told us that we were cleaning ourselves up and make it possible to take our wives to heaven with us, that they were suppose to be there when we got there. We cleansed ourselves by attending the meetings, reading the Bible and listening to spirituals. We were suppose to stay at his house from Friday until Monday, that the world was suppose to end Monday but it didn't end. He didn't say how he knew the world was going to end, he just told us to do right and follow instructions and that he could do what he had to do. We had wine sacrifice, where it's written in the Bible, drink no more water but drink wine for thy stomach's sake. That was wine sacrifice. We used marijuana but not for narcotics sake, we was taught that it was an herb.
Q: Have you ever seen Lindberg Sanders use any type of force on the members of the group?
A: Yes, he used a stick, a black stick that he kept there, it was almost like a police blackjack, black wood. He never used it on me because I always stayed in a corner and kept quiet. I called him a lie once and he said if I ever called him a lie again he was going to kick me in my ass, so I never called him a lie.

10:10am

A.C. Wharton, and a second attorney from the Public Defender's office came to the Violent Crimes office and asked to speak with T.C. Smith. The interview was stopped and the attorneys were allowed to speak with Smith.

A few minutes later, Smith told Anderson that he did not wish to make a statement or sign the partial statement already taken. Anderson wrote at the bottom of the statement refused to sign, 10:25am.

Smith was taken back to the jail and later released without charge.

The seven bodies had been placed side by side on the floor of the morgue. The hideousness of the gunshot ravaged bodies were made more so by the bright lights in the room.

Sgt. Landers, the same officer who had photographed Bobby Hester's body, had arrived back at Shannon Street shortly after the bodies had been transported. Lt. Wilson told him to go back to the morgue to photograph and do wound charts on the seven. Sgt. J. D. Douglas and Sgt. S. E. Chambers, who were with the Violent Crimes Bureau, were to assist.

Landers took photos of the bodies and in particular the clothing and wounds. Douglas and Chambers made wound charts of each suspect's injuries.

All clothing was collected, placed separately in brown paper sacks, to prevent cross contamination, and tagged in the property room.

Photographs were taken and shown to T. C. Smith, before his release from custody. Smith identified the seven men to investigators.

CHAPTER 34
Hester's Autopsy

January 13th, 1983
10:00am

D r. Harlan looked at the preliminary medical examiner's report on the table beside him. He glanced at the ghost white figure laying nude on the stainless steel table. The blood that had covered the body earlier had been washed off. Two assistants stood near a smaller stainless steel table that was lined with gleaming cutting tools. Beside the smaller table set a meat cutter's scales.

Harlan's eyes moved down the page.

Name of the decedent: R.S. Hester, Race: W, Sex: M, age: 34, Home Address: Clearbrook.

Narrative Summary: W M 34, beaten to death at 2239 Shannon while being held by 7 male blacks in a hostage situation. Victim was a Memphis Police officer(See multiple additional charts). The remaining 7 male blacks were shot in a shootout with Memphis Police.

The autopsy lasted approximately 65 minutes. Harlan would issue an official report, made public on February 4th, 1983.

(Following is Dr. Harlan's report, with portions omitted for brevity's sake. Some of the medical language has been modified for better understanding.)

Cause of Death

Multiple lacerations to head, multiple contusions to head, subarachnoid hemorrhage, cerebral cortical contusions with lacerations, compound fracture of nose.

Narrative of Findings

This 34 year old white male received multiple blows to the head from a blunt object, which produced multiple lacerations of the scalp, contusions, compound fracture of the nose, through-and through lacerations of upper and lower lips, fracture of a tooth, recent subarachnoid hemorrhage, recent bruises and tears(used as verb, meaning to separate by force)(contusions and lacerations) of cerebral cortex and death.

Full and fixed rigor mortis, with fixed livor mortis is present at the time of examination. There is absence of green discoloration of the skin and finger pads are smooth, of normal texture, consistency, and color at examination.

The facts are consistent with death 12-24 hours prior to examination.

The changes in the brain are consistent with death having occurred 8-12 hours following the time of injury. This also is consistent with the type, quantity, and characteristics of the gastric contents identified and the gastric contents pH.

On the basis of historical data and autopsy data, it can be reasonably stated that death occurred in the interval from 0400-0900 hours (4am-9am) January 12th, 1983.

Starting from the top of the head, Hester's injuries were as follows,

1. laceration to the bone, at the upper top, right portion of the head,

2. abrasions to top right of head along hair line,

3. laceration, to the bone, on right side of head,

4. laceration-avulsion on right side of face near right eye,

5. contusion around right eye,

6. compound fracture to nose with laceration,

7. abrasion to right cheek,

8./ **9.** through-and-through lacerations to upper and lower lip,

10. / **11.** two lacerations to left upper side of head extending to lower, left, rear of head, just above left ear,

12. laceration above left eye,

13. contusion around left eye,

14. abrasion to left of left eye,

15. laceration to left and below left eye,

16. laceration to left, rear, middle of head,

17. laceration with avulsion, at right, rear, lower part of head, **18.** abrasions to front of neck,

19. abrasion to upper left chest,

20. contusion to upper left chest, left of and above left nipple,

21. pale green depression to right, under side, of wrist,

22. red contusions with yellow margins on upper right thigh,

23. pale green depression to left, under side, of wrist,

24. / **25.** purple contusions to upper, inner thigh near genitals and on inner thigh just below the first,

26. / **27.** two puncture / stab wounds to lower right leg just below knee, one above the other,

28. / **29** / **30** / **31** / **32** / **33.** abrasions on left and right knees and area above and below both knees,

34. avulsion / laceration to left index finger nail tip,

35. laceration to left elbow,

36. lacerations to right elbow,

37. pale green depression to top left wrist,

38. abrasion to upper left hand,

39. pale green depression to top right wrist,
40. / **41.** abrasions to upper right hand.

Sgt. Hollie trudged up the steps and in through the front doors of the Justice Center from Poplar Avenue. He walked to the set of four elevators that serviced floors seven through twelve. As he waited for an elevator, he glanced at attorneys and citizens boarding another set of four elevators for floors two through seven.

Three minutes later, he was in the Violent Crimes, eleventh floor office. Twenty old brown wooden desks, recently moved from the old police building, sat atop newly laid desert brown carpet. Hollie squeezed between desks as he poured himself a cup of coffee and walked to his desk.

Steam rose from the coffee while he rubbed his eyes. He rolled the departmental form into the typewriter. He stared at the single piece of paper laying in the typewriter, and took a deep breath.

He began to type in the information, for the Homicide Bureau Memphis Police Department, Homicide Analysis Sheet.

District 127; R&I number 83/01/13/2672; Homicide Number 14/5296; Victims Name, Hester, Robert S., Sex M, Race W, Age 34, B of I Number, DNA (Does not Apply), Corpus Delicti Witness, Capt. Josh Randle; Relationship, Worked together.

Date of Occurrence, **1/13/83**; Time, **3:13a**; Day of the Week, **Thurs.**; Time **3:13am**, Pronounced By **Dr. Pervis Milnor**; Date of Death, **1/13/83**, Pronounced At, **2239 Shannon**; Weapon Used(Specify Type), **5-cell flashlight**.

Hollie glanced at his notes while he typed. He had never had so much trouble filling out the form before. The shock of what had happened was still sinking in. This was some real shit Hollie thought as he continued to type.

Offender at Scene, Yes **X** No _; Offender Identified Through Investigation, **Yes**; Offender Taken Into Custody, (**DOA**);

Date, **1/13/83**; Time, **4:40am**; Offender Surrendered, **DNA**; Admission, **DNA**; Death of Offender, **X**;

Intoxicants Involved _ Yes **X** NO; Offender Arrested By **DNA**; First Officers On Scene, **SEE NARRATIVE**; Relationship Victim/ Offender, **X** Home; **X** Other Specify (**Possible Larceny Suspect**).

Evidence: **Weapon used to brutally beat Officer recovered, witness statements**; Evidence To Medical Examiner, **Yes**; Evidence To FBI, **No** T.B.I.;

Brief Account of Facts,

On January 11, 1983, Patrolman Robert S. Hester was taken hostage by the seven male black defendants. This incident took place at approximately 9:15pm and occurred at 2239

Shannon. Ptlm. Hester's partner, Ptlm. R. Schwill was able to escape after being wounded by gunfire. Tact Officers surrounded the house and the Negotiation Team attempted to talk the seven male blacks out for approximately 30 hours. On Jan. 13, 1983 the decision was made for the Tact Officers to assault the house in an attempt to free Ptlm. Hester. At 3:05am, on January 13, 1983, six Tact officers assaulted the house and during the assault all seven male black defendants were fatally wounded. It was also learned that Ptlm. Hester had been brutally beaten and was dead on the scene. For further information see Shoot Team File 02-83 through 12-83.

Reporting Officer, Sgt. D.R. Hollie; IBM 3323.

Hollie got up from his desk, walked over to the Homicide Ledger and placed the form inside. Hester was the fourteenth homicide victim of 1983.

4:00pm

Officers Billy Robbins and Fred Cohn left the Lieutenants office at the West Precinct and walked out into the back parking lot. Five minutes later they parked their cruiser and walked down the ramp into the morgue. Dr. O.C. Smith was charting wounds on the seven males from the Shannon House.

Robbins and Cohn worked the four to twelve shift at the West Precinct but had been told by their Lieutenant to report to the morgue and stay there until relieved sometime around midnight.

The police department had received threats that an attempt would be made to take the seven bodies from the morgue. Until the bodies were released to the families, they would be under police protection.

Robbins looked at the seven bodies and noticed the large amount of hair that covered each of them. He stared with morbid fascination at the horrible head wounds suffered by the seven suspects. He brought his hand and pinched his nose shut in a vain attempt to block out the heavy stench that hung in the air.

Everywhere he looked there were more bodies. Several other victims who had succumb to death in one manner or another. The rate of bodies coming in each day from all over the city was greater than the staff's ability to autopsy them and get them back out.

Because of the high profile nature of Shannon Street, the other bodies awaiting their turn under the knife would have to wait a little longer.

Hester's body had been removed several hours before.

Wayne Hightower and Dennis Wilson stood in the lobby of the Memphis Funeral Home on Union. The two North Precinct officers had been asked by Director Holt to represent the police department in overseeing arrangements for the funeral of Hester. The two had to determine among other things if the body was viewable.

Hightower and Wilson were led through a hallway and down a set of stairs to the basement of the funeral home and into a small room. Lying on a table was the nude body of Hester.

Hightower felt sick to his stomach as he looked at the pale white body of his former partner. His hand reached out to the wall for support as he fought the urge to vomit. Finally, he turned and walked from the room without saying a word. He headed up the stairs and out into the cold evening air.

With trembling hands he lit a cigarette and stared up at the stars.

The body was not viewable.

CHAPTER 35
Seven Autopsies

The Shelby County Medical Examiner's office and the police department had a conference concerning the wounds and cause of death of the seven suspects. Dr. C. W. Harlan, Dr. Stafford and the Medical Examiner Jerry Francisco sat at the conference table. On the table lay charts and diagrams of the seven dead men. Inspector Jackson, Captain Hasty and Captain Clyde Keenan sat at the table and listened to the presentation.

Harlan included miniature clay models showing bullet trajectory in relation to each suspect.

(Following is Dr. Harlan's reports, with portions omitted for brevity's sake. Some of the medical language has been modified for better understanding).

A-1- **Larnell Sanders, 26 years of age**:
Gunshot wound to head, entry above and to the right, of right eye, 66 inches from heel, bullet traversing brain, right and left frontal lobes, bullet fragments recovered. This gunshot caused multiple skull fractures.
Gunshot wound to chest, entry at right chest near and just above nipple, 53 inches above heel.
Gunshot wound to middle back, 53 inches above heel;

Gunshot wound to right middle back, 52 ½ inches above heel. Bullets traversing right lung, thyroid, esophagus, aorta, left subclavian artery, trachea, left lung, multiple bullet fragments recovered, bullets traversing right to left.

The gunshot wounds were described as high velocity small caliber wounds with three being to the chest and one to the head.
Cause of Death: Multiple gunshot wounds to chest and head.
Larnell Sanders showed to have no alcohol in his blood stream. Positive for tetrahydrocannabinol which is the active ingredient in marijuana.

B-2 - Michael Coleman, 18 years of age:
Gunshot wound to left face/head, gunshot wound to right palm, gunshot wound to right forearm, gunshot wound to left lower extremity and gunshot wound to brain.
Gunshot wound to left lower extremity at the left knee, 18 inches above heel, causing fracture of left tibia, left fibula fracture, laceration extends into the knee joint space.
Gunshot wound to right forearm bullet traversed forearm and bone fragments exiting via several lacerations of forearm.
Gunshot wound to left face was 66 ½ inches above heel, bullet traversing left to right, anterior (front) to posterior (back), inferior (down) to superior (up).
The head shot caused multiple skull fractures, multiple cerebral and cerebellar cortical lacerations and contusions, multiple bone fragments and metal fragments in cerebrum.
Cause of Death: Gunshot wound to head.
Coleman had no alcohol in his blood stream. Positive for tetrahydrocannabinols.

C-3 - David Lee Jordan Sr, 29 years of age:

Gunshot wound to left arm, shotgun wound to left head, laceration of brain, aortic and coronary atherosclerosis, incision/laceration right forehead.

Gunshot wound to left arm, 47 ½ inches above heel, traversing anterior (front) to posterior (rear), superior (up) to inferior (down) - metal fragment recovered 47 ½ inches above heel in / at entrance wound and larger metal fragment recovered 47 inches to heel in subcutaneous tissue.

Shotgun wound to left head, 62 to 66 inches above heel, one spurious shotgun pellet wound 63 inches above heel posterior through skull and brain.

There were multiple skull fractures - compound and comminuted - fragments absent from body, multiple lacerations and maceration of brain with aspiration of blood, pulmonary (lung) congestion, visceral (abdomen) congestion.

Cause of Death: Shotgun wound to head.

Jordan had no alcohol in blood stream. Positive for tetrahydrocannabinols.

D-4 - Cassell Alonzo Harris, 21 years of age:

Gunshot wound to head, entry right occipital/mastoidal region (lower right back of head), producing brain injury, aspiration of blood into lungs.

Gunshot wound to head 64 inches above heel, traversing posterior (rear) to anterior (front), right to left, multiple fragments recovered. Disruption of cerebellum and brain stem, extensive skull fractures.

Cause of Death: Gunshot wound to head as a result of a high velocity, small caliber gunshot wound to the head producing injury to the brain and death.

Harris had no alcohol in his blood stream. Positive for tetrahydrocannabinol.

E-5 - Earl Thomas, 20 years of age:
Multiple gunshot wounds to abdomen, chest, left forearm and head, multiple myxomata, right ventricle heart, bilateral hemothorax.
Gunshot wound with entry at left upper quadrant abdomen 46 ½ above heel, traversing left lobe liver, right diaphragm, right lower lobe lung through right intercostal space 5-6 inches above heel, numerous minute fragments of bullet causing injury to stomach, pancreas, left diaphragm, left lower lobe lung, pericardium, right atrium and ventricle, heart. Direction is anterior (front) to posterior (rear), inferior (down) to superior (up), left to right.
Gunshot wound with entry at posterior (rear) aspect left forearm fracturing humerus, radius and ulna with multiple overstretch lacerations of forearm, to exit at left forearm where fragment recovered and retained, unlabeled. Bullet re-entry at gunshot wound right anterior chest 52 ½ inches above heel, recovered subcutaneously right anterior (front) chest 54 ½ inches above heel. Direction is anterior (front) to posterior (rear), inferior (down) to superior (up), left to right.
Gunshot grazing wound at right upper arm and lateral aspect right chest 53 ½ to 55 inches above heel with disruption of subcutaneous and muscle tissue only, bullet not recovered. Direction is anterior (front) to posterior (rear).
Gunshot wound with entry at right side of face with large excavated defect 62 to 63 ½ inches above heel, traversing skull with production of secondary missiles to enter brain, with extensive disruption, fragments recovered. Direction is anterior (front) to posterior (rear), inferior (down) to superior (up), left to right.

Cause of Death: Multiple high velocity, small caliber gunshot wounds to the head, chest and abdomen, producing injury to the liver, diaphragm, lungs, stomach, pancreas, heart, left humerus, radius and ulna, brain, bleeding and death.

Thomas had no alcohol in his blood stream. Positive for tetrahydrocannabinol.

F-6 - Lindberg Sanders, 49 years of age:

Gunshot wounds to left wrist, head, multiple fractures, graze to head, gunshot wound to head, multiple skull fractures.

Gunshot wound to left wrist (inside), entry causing fracture of left radius, exit at (outer) wrist with bullet traversing volar to extensor surfaces, bullet fragments recovered.

Gunshot wound graze to left side of head (even with and to rear of eye brow), 65 inches above heel.

Gunshot wound to back of upper head with entry 69 ½ inches above heel with bullet fragments and bone fragments traversing brain, fragments recovered traversing anterior(front) to posterior(rear), right to left, superior (up) to inferior (down), partial exit at (back of head down and to left of entry) 63 inches above heel. Multiple skull fractures.

Cause of Death: Gunshot wound to head.

Sanders had alcohol in his blood stream. Positive for tetrahydrocannabinol.

G-7 - Andrew Houston, 19 years of age:

Gunshot wound to left hand, gunshot wound to left flank, gunshot wounds to head.

Gunshot wound to left hand entry (top of left hand at base of middle finger) exit at outer side of hand below pinkie finger.

Gunshot wound to head entry in left cheek 61 inches above heel bullet traversing brain fragments recovered traversing anterior(front) to posterior(rear). Bullet fragments at left cheek, mouth and right cheek traversed base of both cerebral hemispheres, separating cerebellum and brainstem from the cerebrum. Multiple skull fractures caused by fragments.

Gunshot wound to head, entry in upper lip 61 inches above heel, bullet traversing mazilla, brain, fragments recovered, traversing anterior (front) to posterior (rear).

Gunshot wound to left flank, entry 41 inches above heel, bullet recovered in posterior subcutaneous tissue 44 inches above heel, traversing left to right, inferior (down) to superior (up) with contusion to left kidney.

Death as a result of three high velocity, small caliber gunshot wounds to the head, producing extensive injury to the brain, separating the cerebellum and brainstem from the cerebrum. The gunshot wounds to the left hand and left flank are consistent with large caliber, .38 caliber, gunshot wounds occurring some 24- 36 hours prior to death. .38 caliber bullet recovered from left flank.

Houston had no alcohol in his blood stream. Positive for tetrahydrocannabinol.

CHAPTER 36
Assault to Murder

January 14th through January 16th, 1983
Security Squad Office

They were rounded up a few each day and brought to the Security Squad office to be questioned. No one was hiding anymore but only a few volunteered to come in. Once located and brought to the office none seemed to have a problem talking about what they were apart of or what they had seen, up to a point. Convenient memories and selective eye sight turned several statements into self-serving double-talk, causing problems for investigators.

Seven men had escaped the house that night, their faithfulness to Lindberg Sanders starting to wavier when Hester and Schwill walked into the house. Their loyalty to Lindberg's cause fled as quickly as they did when the bullets began to fly.

One, T.C. Smith, had been interviewed and released from jail. Six more men, who had also been present in the house, would have to be located and interviewed. Some would give statements as witnesses, one would tell his story as a suspect.

By January 14th, the police knew many things about Lindberg Sanders and the other six men killed inside the house. One question still remained and they hoped, through the long process of interviews with the 'cult' members, they might find an answer.

They wanted to know why.

(In the following statements some questions and answers were removed for brevity sake. What is reprinted is the actual text from the statements).

Statement of **James Murphy Jr., 29** years of old.

Sgt. Collier sipped his coffee as he waited for Robbins to finish typing the heading on the witness statement. Collier read the witness his Miranda Rights off the statement, then began asking questions.

Q: Mr. Murphy, do you know or are you acquainted with Lindberg Sanders?

A: I did know him.

Q: What is your association with Lindberg Sanders?

A: I go over to his house and read the Bible every now and then.

Q: On January 11ᵗʰ, 1983, Tuesday, was you at Lindberg Sanders home?

A: Yes.

Q: How long have you known Lindberg Sanders?

A: Five or six years.

Q: How did you get acquainted with him?

A: I got acquainted with his sons first, go fishing and stuff, then I got to know him.

Q: What was your purpose for being at Lindberg Sanders' home on Tuesday, 1/11/83?

A: I rode down with Reginald.

Q: Why did you and Reginald go to Sanders' home?

A: To read the Bible.

Q: During the time period that you have been acquainted with Lindberg Sanders have you ever heard him make any type statement regarding his likes or dislikes for policemen?

A: He told me he had some trouble with police years ago and they busted his head, or something like that. That he did not care for them and did not want them coming to his house. I've heard him say God will take care of whoever messes with him.

Q: Do you know what he meant by the statement God will take care of whoever messes with him?

A: Meaning that God would do all the fighting for him or whatever he had to do. He always referred to the police as being the devil.

Q: After Michael received the phone call and then made the phone call back to someone, did this seem to upset Sanders?

A: Lindberg, to me a little bit it seemed to upset him. It scared me, because he said you call those folks back and tell them where you at and you ain't did nothing. Also tell them where you at and if they want to come over here, to come on.

Q: Exactly where were you in the house when the police came to the door?

A: Everybody was in the front. There were about three or four of us sitting in the floor around the table.

Q: How many policemen came to the door?

A: One came in and was talking with Michael and the other one was standing back at the door. So it was two policemen.

Q: What did the policeman say to Michael?

A: He was saying something and then Berg started talking to the policeman. Him and the policeman was passing words back and forth, like they was arguing. Berg gave the policeman a piece of paper or something and a scuffle broke out between Berg and one of the policeman.

Then everything in the house went crazy and I ran out the back door.

Q: After Lindberg started scuffling with the policeman, how many of the others in the house jumped on the policeman?

A: I don't know but it was a whole bunch of them.

Q: Did you ever hear any gunshots?

A: Yea, as I jumped the fence I heard some gunshots. That's what shook me up. I went on around to my sister's house, I didn't know what was going on.

Q: During all the years you have known Lindberg did he ever tell you why he had such a hatred for policemen?

A: Yes, Because they had done took him somewhere and busted his head and they busted it to make it feel like ground beef and that they really killed him but he had come to life like little Jesus and he couldn't die again. He thought all the policemen were devils.

Q: Why do you think Lindberg reacted the way he did when the policeman came to his house that night?

A: He just didn't like him and I noticed in the past two weeks his attitude changed and he got real mean. I didn't understand what was going on.

Q: When was the last time that Lindberg told you that the world was coming to an end?

A: Last Monday.

Q: What was his reaction when the world didn't come to an end on Monday? Was he pissed off or mad?

A: Like I say he was getting mean.

Q: Did you ever know Lindberg to have a lot of guns around the house?

A: Not lately, but before, I know'd him he use to have a lot of guns, gun rack and all.

Q: You have stated before in this statement that Lindberg had hatred for a policeman. Did he ever specify whether he hated white policemen specifically, or was it just policemen in general? Color did not make any difference with him as far as policemen went. Is that correct?

A: Police were police.

Q: Do you think that the police officers that came into the house conducted themselves in a professional manner?

A: Yes, they did. They asked for Michael and said there was going to have to be some attitude changes because Berg was real loud with them.

Q: From what you observed when the police officers came in the house, who started the fight?

A: Lindberg is the one who started the fight by his actions towards the police officers.

Q: Besides Lindberg Sanders and Michael Coleman, what other people did you observe to take part in the fight when it first started?

A: I'm not sure, but I saw five or six pounce on him.

Melvin Davis, 19 years old, looked up and across the table as Sgt. Wheeler cleared his throat.

Q: Melvin, do you know Lindberg Sanders?

A: Yes, I know him.

Q: How do you know him?

A: I am a member of his religious group.

Q: Were you at Lindberg Sanders' house on Tuesday, January 11, 1983?

A: No.

Q: When was the last time you saw Lindberg Sanders?

A: Monday evening.

Q: What was the purpose for going to Lindberg Sanders' house?

A: There was a meeting over at his house.

Q: What was the purpose of the meeting?

A: He said the world was suppose to end on Monday.

Q: Did he say when the world was suppose to come to an end?

A: Monday, he said it was suppose to end on Monday.

Q: How many people were at Lindberg's house when you got there Monday?
A: About 16.
Q: Did your group have a particular name?
A: Everybody called us crazy so we named ourselves the Lunch Bunch, we was out to lunch.
Q: Who was in charge of the group?
A: Lindberg Sanders.
Q: Did Lindberg call himself anything as being head of the group?
A: He was the elder.

Q: Explain in detail the teachings of Lindberg Sanders to your group?
A: It was white man couldn't go to heaven but the black man could. The Bible was made particular for the black man but not the white man. We couldn't eat pork or drink clear water. Don't commit fornication, couldn't shave, it was alright to smoke marijuana, he called it herb from the fields. It was just the Holy Bible, everything in the Bible was basic.
Q: Have you ever had a disagreement with Lindberg over his teachings?
A: Several times.
Q: How would he react when you disagreed with him?
A: He'd fly off real bad. He felt like if we had anything wrong he could correct us.
Q: Did Lindberg consider white people beast in his teachings?
A: Yes, another heathen.
Q: What would his reaction be if you associated with them?
A: I would be as him, a beast too.
Q: Did he ever make any statements to you that he did not like policemen?
A: He disliked policemen, yeah.

Q: Did he ever mention the name of any policemen that he disliked more than others?

A: He said all policemen were the same, white or black.

Q: If someone would have entered Lindberg's house while the group was there would the group do anything to this person that Lindberg told them to?

A: Yes.

Q: If the group had got in trouble what would Lindberg think of someone running out on the group?

A: I can't think of no name but I know he would have a name for them, terrible I know that.

Q: Were the ones killed at Lindberg's house avid followers?

A: Yes, avid followers of Lindberg. Lindberg said he was following as Jesus and we were following Lindberg, so we were all following Jesus.

Q: Did the group look upon Lindberg as God?

A: As a King, yes.

Q: If some of the group would have wanted to come out of the house on Shannon Street could Lindberg have talked them out of coming out?

A: Yes.

Q: Were the other people more hard core followers of Lindberg's than yourself?

A: Yes, because they had more years.

Q: How many followers do you know that Lindberg had?

A: Somewhere in the 20s.

Q: What was Lindberg's belief about death?

A: That the only reason you would die was God killed you, that if you were doing what the book said the said you couldn't die.

Q: Did Lindberg believe that any human being on earth could kill him?

A: No.

Collier had finished his oral interview with **29 year old Reginald McCray** as he looked over his notes. He began asking questions when he heard Robbins stop typing.

Q: Mr. McCray, do you know or are you acquainted with Lindberg Sanders?

A: I know him.

Q: What is your association with him?

A: I was raised in the neighborhood, went to Shannon School with his kids, Larnell and Lucinda.

Q: On Tuesday, Jan. 11, 1983, was you in Lindberg Sanders' house?

A: Yes sir.

Q: What time did Melvin, Benjamin and Tim leave the house?

A: It was early that day. We all had left. I had taken Melvin, Tim and Ben home and I came back by there and stayed.

Q: From Friday, January 7th until Tuesday, January 11th, what did everybody do in the house of Lindberg Sanders' at 2239 Shannon?

A: Well from the time I got there Saturday morning, smoked and read the Bible all day and drank wine.

Q: Did any of you ever sleep during this period?

A: Yes sir, we would, like I say we drank wine, read the Bible, smoke dope, we would sleep from time to time.

Q: What was the physical condition and mental condition of yourself, and the other people in the house Tuesday evening when the police arrived?

A: David, Lindberg, Larnell, Earl, the ones that was still in there. Right before the police came everything was peaceful. But the answer to your question, we was all high as hell.

Q: Have you ever seen Pete with a snub nose, chrome plated, 38 pistol?

A: No sir, like I say Peter's daddy is my daddy.

Q: Did Lindberg Sanders teach or preach that we're all one family as a unit and you will stick together even until death?

A: Yes.

Q: Who answered the door to let the police officers in?

A: Lindberg, he answered the door, he said come in.

Q: Where did the police station themselves in when they got inside the house?

A: One was at the door, closing the door behind him, the other one was right in front of him standing there talking to Lindberg, by the fireplace.

Q: Who was the officer directing his conversation to?

A: At first Lindberg Sanders and then Lindberg said, this is the guy you're looking for and pointed to Michael Coleman. Then, was when the heavy set officer asked Michael about the purse snatch and Michael replied, I ain't did a goddamned thing and then that's when Lindberg said, well arrest us all for shoplifting and told us we all was going out to line up by the car. The heavy set officer, I'm still laying on the floor watching, said we're gonna have to change some attitudes in here. Then Lindberg said, no, we all gonna get arrested and go downtown and started out the door. Lindberg, Michael, David, Larnell, JuJu, Cassell, and Tyrone, I believe they got up and started heading towards the door and then the heavy set officer was outside with Lindberg and the slim officer, pushed, stopped them at the door and I don't know which one of the seven in the crowd it was started to push back. I'm still laying on the floor and I saw them push back against the officer which provoked the fight. This is when me, Jackie and T.C. got up off the floor and moved back to the opening towards the rear of the house.

Q: After you got up and moved to the rear of the living room what did you observe then?

A: I observed Michael Coleman and about three others with the slim officer go through the bedroom door, right to the left of the

277

front door. The heavy set officer and Lindberg and one in that crowd, I think Tyrone, was wrestling out the door, out the front door.

Then I heard a lick in the bedroom, somebody hitting somebody where they had the slim officer at. Almost instantly I heard a shot in the front where the heavy set officer and Lindberg and other Tyrone was. Then I looked back in the living room and the heavy set officer was sitting down in front of the fireplace, Tyrone was standing in front of the door which is now closed, front door and Lindberg is sitting on the couch right beside the front door in the living room with the officer's pistol in his hand. I then heard the officer ask Lindberg what the hell is going on and about the same time this officer, heavy set one, made a grab for the gun in Lindberg's hand. Then Tyrone, David and Earl grabbed the officer and pulled him back and sat him down by the fireplace.

Then I looked into the bedroom and I saw the slim officer on the floor with his head towards the east bedroom wall and Michael Coleman and JuJu were beating on him. I also saw Larnell with the slim officer's gun, standing by the door in the bedroom where the slim officer was at. I did notice that the slim officer was holding his police radio with both hands up against his chest. I don't know if he was trying to talk on it or what.

Q: While you were still on the scene, did any other officer come to the house?
A: I didn't see the officers but when the door was kicked open I heard, alright you mother fuckers break it up and then pow.
Q: What did you do then?
A: I turned and ran out the back door on the south side and I went over the fence.
Q: Do you think the two police officers who made the call conducted themselves in a professional manner?
A: Yes sir, about as professional as you can be.

Q: From your observation as to what happened inside the house, who provoked this fight?
A: I'd have to say Lindberg, really Michael.

Jackie Robinson Young, 25 years old listened as Wheeler read him his rights.

Mr. Young, you are not under arrest at this time, however I will advise you of your rights before taking a statement from you...
Q: How do you know Lindberg Sanders?
A: He is my cousin and I know him from when he was working construction jobs and through his sons.
Q: State in detail everything that occurred after you went to Lindberg Sanders' house.

Robinson began by recounting what had transpired from Saturday morning through Tuesday evening.

Then he went into what happened when the phone rang on Tuesday evening, January 11th.
A: As Lindberg was talking the phone rang. He answered the phone and the police were on the phone asking about Michael and then Michael got on the phone, talked to the police for a short while and hung it up. Then Mr. Sanders got angry with Michael and told him if you didn't do anything why did you hang up and know you didn't do nothing. So he told him to call home first to see if the police were still there. The police were not there and he told him to call the police station. Michael did that and told them where he was and where to send the police car.
The police got there and started questioning Michael.
Michael said he ain't did a damn thing. Then the policeman said, he got on his radio and he said some attitudes are going to change in here. He called for a backup. Then he got Michael

and took him out. Then all the rest of the men said we are all going to jail. Then the officer, the other officer stopped us at the door, then Michael grabbed, Mr. Sanders was ahead of everybody when we said we was all going to jail. Then the officer grabbed Mr. Sanders and said mother fucker you come here and had Mr. Sanders by his collar, took Mr. Sanders on outside.

Then Michael grabbed the other police that was holding us because he was outside. When Michael grabbed him, JuJu grabbed him and David grabbed him and took him in the bedroom to the left of the door. Then I heard the policeman that was in the bedroom, I heard, hit him with the flashlight. After that I heard the police call for help and after he called for help he was asking them what did he do, Michael, JuJu and David, he asked them what did he do. Then I came through the room where they were and I saw them take the radio from him and then after I went into the kitchen Lonnie (Larnell) came out with his gun.

Then I stepped into the hallway beside Lonnie with the gun and when I stood there I saw the police try to get the gun from Mr. Sanders, they had already brought him back in then, then I was hearing the backup, that came. I heard him kicking the door. I didn't stay after I heard that. Before I could get out there were several shots fired before I got to the back door and as I went on out the back door through the fence I knocked some boards out of the fence I heard T.C. say man, I'm hit and I said come on man, let's go to my house.

We went and jumped a few fences and I said let's just stop and lay down for a minute man. We waited for a few minutes then I took him to my mother's house, then he called his mother and he left and went home. I was going to stay there and wait for you all to come, but after I seen what they had said on TV and we were trying to kill the police, I know better, I wasn't trying to kill nobody. When I called my mother last night I said I know because Pete has told me that they had questioned him and he told them the same thing that I said. Then this morning I heard from Reginald's sister, she said if we didn't come down they would put out a warrant for our arrest.

Q: After Michael called the police to the house, what did Lindberg Sanders tell you all about leaving before the police got there?

A: He said if the police come here some of you all is going to get somewhere. He was talking to everybody, but he said he already knew if the police come there to the house you all are going to get somewhere because you are scared.

Q: Did you have a feeling by the statement that Lindberg made to you that something was going to happen when the police got to the house?

A: I did know what, but I had this feeling. I couldn't think what he was talking about.

Q: What mood was Lindberg Sanders in after Michael called the police to the house?

A: He was angry at Michael because Michael didn't do it right the first time the police called, Michael didn't talk to them right. He was telling Michael if you hadn't done nothing why did you do that if you knowed you hadn't did anything.

Q: When the police officers arrived at the house what position in the house did they take?

A: One of the police were standing in front of the fireplace. The other one was close by the two doors, the bedroom door and the living room door.

Q: What had Lindberg said to make the officer grab him and not everybody else?

A: Mr. Sanders had some papers in his hands, he tried to show them to the bigger of the officers. Mr. Sanders said something to the police that made the police mad and the policeman said some attitudes were going to change. I have forgot what he said.

Q: Did Lindberg get real angry with the police because they would not look at the papers he was trying to show them?
A: Yes, he did.
Q: What did Lindberg do or say to the officers at this time?
A: He got real loud, Lindberg did.
Q: Who struck the first blow?
A: Michael Coleman.
Q: After Michael grabbed the officer that was standing at the door, who else grabbed this officer?

A: JuJu grabbed him, Cassell was there too, David was there and Earl. I believe it may have been more but I didn't see who else. I moved out of the way.
Q: How many times did you see the officer in the bedroom get hit and what was he hit with?
A: He was hit with a flashlight, 3 times that I seen. He was getting hit with fists, if they had anything else I didn't see that. Didn't nobody hit him with nothing but the flashlight but Michael.
Q: How hard was Michael hitting the officer?
A: He was hitting him pretty hard but the first one was the hardest one of all. I heard the first one.
Q: You stated earlier that Tyrone, Cassell and Lindberg Sanders had one officer in the living room and JuJu, Lonnie and Michael Coleman were in the bedroom. Where were the other people that were in the house with you at this time?
A: I saw Fred sitting on the couch in the living room. Reginald was in the back of the house, T.C. was in the bathroom, Joe was in the back, everybody in the back was ready to run. I wasn't in the back but I was ready to go. Pete was in the front room but he wasn't on the officer. I believe Earl was still in the bedroom with the short officer, David was in the living room, I was in the hall, Lonnie was in the hall.

Q: Do you know if the officer that was in the living room was shot while he was at the house?
A: Tyrone told me later that the officer that they had in the yard was shot in the yard.
Q: Do you know where this officer was shot, what part of the body?
A: The face.
Q: Does the organization that you belong to have a name?

A: This what people call us, the Lunch Bunch, saying we are crazy, out to lunch.
Q: Had Lindberg told you all that anything unusual was going to happen?
A: Yes, the earth was going to catch on fire. It was said Monday, but then Mr. Sanders told us no man knows the hour.
Q: What was Lindberg's feeling on death?
A: He told us he had been through that, had died and come back and he wasn't going to die no more.

Fred Davis, 28 years old, massaged his cramping stomach as he sat in the little room in the Security Squad office.
Q: Mr. Davis, do you know or are you acquainted with Lindberg Sanders?
A: Yes, I know him. I've known him for about a year and a half.
Q: What is your association with him?
A: Well, we just friends, just fellow Bible readers.
Q: Was you at his house at his house on Tuesday, January 11th, 1983?
A: Yes, I was.
Q: For the five days and nights that you all were at Lindberg's house, what all did you do?
A: Well, we read a little, talked, if anybody wanted to, you know, smoke a joint we did that, Mrs. Sanders brought some wine and we drunk that. Listened to the music on WLOK.

Q: Getting back to Tuesday evening, January 11, 1983, exactly where was you in the house when the policemen came?

A: I was sitting in the doorway of the hall between the living room and the bathroom.

Q: Can you explain the exact location of the other people in the house when the police came in?

A: T.C., Earl, Mike and David Jordan was on the couch by the front door and Pete, Tyrone, Jackie and Reginald was on the love seat and Lonnie, JuJu, Cassell on the extension of the love seat on the south wall of the living room. Lindberg was sitting on the arm of a chair on the south wall of the living room. Joe was standing by me on the east wall of the living room.

Q: When the police got to the house and knocked on the door who answered the door?

A: Didn't nobody get up, Lindberg said come on in. He seen the car through the window.

Q: I will show you a spread of MPD B of I photographs of police officers and see if you can identify the first officers that come in the house?

A: Number 7939(Schwill) and 3434(Hester).

Q: Exactly what happened when these officers come in?

A: The officers entered, 7939 asked if there was a call for them and Berg asked them did y'all have a warrant for Mike and they said they didn't know. That they had got a call to come to this address about a disturbance I think they said, something like that. Then Lindberg asked them was they looking for Mike and they said they didn't know, all they know was they was supposed to come to this address for some type disturbance.

Lindberg told them that they had got a call saying that Mike had snatched a pocket book and they had called once but he wasn't at home and his brother had balled down there and said the police was at the house looking for him. Ben called Mike and said the police had ben looking for him for purse snatching, and that he wanted them to call them and let them know where he was so that they wouldn't think he was hiding from them. Between them talking, they started shouting at each other. Lindberg and Officer 7939. Then he stopped talking to him and said where is Mike and Mike had already stood up and was standing right beside officer 7939. Him and Mike started talking, then officer 7939 said well come on with us and Lindberg said well, I'll go with him and Lindberg and officer 7939 exchanged a few more harsh words and the officer 7939 said well do everybody in this house feel the same way, want to go with him and they said yea, we'll go with him. Officer 7939 grabbed Mike in the collar and pulled him out the door.

Everybody was following him out the door because were all gonna go downtown with him. As officer 7939 was leaving, he said there's gonna be some attitude change around here and he got on the police and called for a back-up. As all of them, officer 7939, Mike and Lindberg was going out the door, Officer 3434 blocked the doorway and I heard a scuffle and I ran, I ran out the back door.

Q: Did you hear anything that sounded like somebody hitting somebody else?

A: As I was leaving the kitchen, going through the den, it sounded like somebody had gotten hit with an object, real hard lick.

Q: After you heard the lick, did you ever hear officer 3434 say anything?

A: Yes, I heard him call out to his partner, he was calling him by his first name. I don't know his name. It sounded as if he was needing help when he called for him.

Q: After Lindberg, Michael and officer 7939 went out the front door, did you ever see them again?

A: No, I never saw them again.

Q: Do you think these two officers conducted themselves in a professional manner?

A: Officer 3434 did, but officer 7939 had sort of an attitude. That's my main reason for getting ready to go.

Tyrone Henley was arrested by uniform officers at 3085 Yale #12 and transported to the Security Squad office and placed in an interview room. Hammers and Collier walked in and closed the door. Hammers read him his Miranda Rights. Henley signed his waiver form agreeing to talk to investigators.

12:55am

After investigators had spoken with Henley they told him he would be charged with Assault with Intent to Commit Murder. Henley agreed to give a formal type written statement.

Tyrone Henley, you are under arrest and will be charged with Assault to Murder, TCA 39-604. This charge growing out of you assaulting Officer R.O. Schwill on Tuesday, January 11, 1983, at 2239 Shannon. You have the right to remain silent. Anything you say can and will be used against you in a court of law. You have the right to have a lawyer, either of your own choice or court appointed if you cannot afford one and to have your lawyer with you during questioning, if you wish.

Q: Do you understand each of these rights I have explained to you?

A: Yes.

Q: Having these rights in mind do you wish to talk to us now?

A: Yes.

Q: Tyrone, do you know Lindberg Sanders?

A: Yes, he's my father.

Q: On Tuesday, January 11, 1983 were you at your father's residence at 2239 Shannon?

A: Yes.

Q: Did he ever tell you or any members of the group that the police had killed him and that he had come back to life as little Jesus and that he couldn't die anymore?

A: Yes he did.

Q: As a result of this incident, did he refer to police as the devil?

A: No, he never came to me and said, Tyrone the police are the devil. I never heard him say that.

Q: Do you know of any mental condition that your father had?

A: Yes, his wife had him committed to a hospital and that's the only one I know of.

Q: Do you know why your father's wife had him committed?

A: No, I don't know why. I had heard that she was under the impression he was gong crazy. That's all I know.

Q: Exactly where were you in the house when the police knocked on the door?

A: I was on the couch on the south wall of the living room.

Q: Do you have any knowledge as to why the police came to Lindberg's house?

A: He received a phone call from Michael's brother and from what I could understand, Ben was telling my father that police were down at the house and were looking for Michael because he had snatched a pocketbook. I heard my father tell Ben that was a lie because Michael had been down there all day and hadn't left the house. Then my father gave Michael the phone and told Michael to talk to the people and explain to them that it couldn't have been him because he was over there. Michael got the phone and was talking on the phone, then the next I know he had hung up the phone. So my father asked him why did he do that and Michael told him that they had hung up the telephone.

So my father told him to pick up the phone and call back, that he didn't have anything to be scared of that he hadn't did anything. Michael called back and they told him that the police had left. He then hung the phone up again and my father told him to call the police and explain to them that the police were at his house looking for him for a purse snatch and he didn't do anything. To tell the police where he was. After Michael called the police and told them, he hung up the phone. The next thing that happened was two police officers were knocking at the door.

Q: I will show you a spread of seven Memphis Police Department B of I photographs of police officers and see if you can identify the first two officers that came in the house.

A: These two officers right here.

Q: For the record, he identified #7939, Officer Ray Schwill and #3434, officer Bob Hester.

You have stated you didn't know either one of these officers when they came to the house, do you know these officers by name now?

A: This one, all I know is Robert Hester and this one is officer Schwill.

Q: How do you know their names now?

A: From listening to the news and seeing their picture on television.

Q: Tyrone, I will ask you to state in your own words and in detail everything that occurred after the two officers entered your father's house?

A: After the two officers knocked on the door and my father told them to come in, after the officers entered, they asked my father did he call them and my father said, didn't y'all call us. Then it started getting loud. The next thing I can remember said was officer Schwill, I heard him say that some attitudes was going to change and he asked for a back-up. Then I saw officer

Schwill grab my father and the other officer grabbed Mike. Then I heard my father say no, y'all attitude is gonna change.

You want me to answer you, but you don't want to answer me. Then I saw the officer shove Michael into the fireplace in the living room, Officer Schwill. Then a lot of commotion broke out and everybody started going towards the officers and grabbed officer Schwill and Hester. I hit officer Schwill with my fist, up side the head or somewhere and the next thing I know after I hit him I had got pushed back by the crowd. There's a big coffee table that hangs, I fell and the next thing I knew my father had one of the officer's pistol, officer Schwill, and I looked around and Lonnie had the other officer's pistol.

Next thing that happened I heard a knock at the door, then I heard kicking at the door. As I heard the door being kicked, I ran out the back door and jumped the fence. When I ran I left my father, he was on the north couch, holding officer Schwill and the pistol. The other officer was in the bedroom and Lonnie had him and his pistol. After I ran, I got over the fence in the next yard, I heard shots. I ran. I kept hearing shots. I ran to my mother's house, she was asleep, I woke her up and told her the police killed my father. She asked was I hurt and I told her no. Later on she took me and my wife and my kids was asleep. I woke her up, my wife and I told her my father was killed. Then I began to look at the news and listen to the radio and that's when I found out that nobody hadn't been killed yet. That's all I did that night.

Q: Who assisted your father in getting officer Schwill's pistol?
A: I don't know.
Q: Who did you see fighting or grabbing a hold of officer Schwill besides your father?
A: Only thing I saw was everybody rushed to the officers.
Q: At anytime during this incident did you fight with officer Schwill in the front yard?

A: No.

Q: Why did you strike officer Schwill and how many times did you strike him?

A: I hit him once and the reason I hit him was because he grabbed my father and was pushing and shoving.

Q: Did you ever grab or strike officer Hester?

A: No, the first time after the fight broke out the next time I saw officer Hester he was in the bedroom and Lonnie had his pistol.

Q: Did you see or hear anyone striking officer Hester while he was in the bedroom?

A: No, I didn't.

Q: After the fight broke out or during the fight did you hear either officer make a statement or say anything?

A: Yea, I heard officer Schwill ask what was the matter and I heard officer Hester ask officer Schwill was he okay and the officer say yes, he was okay. That's the only statement I heard.

Q: Did you ever hear either officer call for help?

A: No.

Q: You stated before that you did see officer Hester in the bedroom, what was his position at the time you saw him?

A: He was just laying down on the floor. Nobody was hitting him and he was conscious.

Q: Did you see any type injuries to officer Hester while he was laying on the floor?

A: Yes, he was bleeding from his head when I saw him, but who hit him I don't know.

Q: You stated earlier in this statement that you saw your father sitting on the couch in the living room with officer Schwill's pistol. Where was officer Schwill at this time?

A: My father had a pistol on him on the floor, on the north wall by the couch, he was crouched up in the corner.

Q: Did you see any injuries on officer Schwill at this time?

A: No.

Q: Was your father saying anything to officer Schwill?

A: No, not that I can recall.

Q: After learning about the hostage situation at 2239 Shannon, involving your father and the other people, did you or why didn't you return and try to help the situation that existed?

A: No, I never did go back. From listening to the news and everything I heard them say they was talking to my father and I had hoped he would come out. But I also knew in my heart that I couldn't talk him out, his wife couldn't talk him out. I knew no one could talk him out.

Tyrone Henley was indicted by the Shelby County Grand Jury on his charge of Assault to Murder and was later sentenced to one year on a reduced charge of Aggravated Assault. He was the only person ever to be charged in the incident.

CHAPTER 37
Media Coverage

Media coverage during the hostage situation had been intense. The three national news agencies, NBC, CBS and ABC had all carried the story. Local television, radio and newspapers provided almost around the clock updates from the scene.

The January 12th front page of the Commercial Appeal featured a picture of the scene just hours after it had begun with the caption above, in bold print, **2 POLICEMAN HURT, 1 HELD HOSTAGE.** The article included a small clip of transcribed radio negotiations between Sanders and Crews.

"I guess he just worked himself down to this state." Lindberg Sander's brother-in-law James McKinney said.

Memphis Police Association President Ray Maples had his own opinion. "I'm utterly disgusted with this whole situation. They seem to be totally disorganized and I think they've waited far too long to make a move. We don't know whether that officer inside is injured or not."

The newspaper told readers that Dorothy Sanders, wife of Lindberg, had been taken to the command post but Lindberg had refused to talk with her.

The Memphis Press-Scimitar, which ran in the evening, was equally dramatic with its headline: **OFFICER HELD HOSTAGE.** Below the headline was a picture of squad cars lining the street in front of the house with related stories and pictures of Hester, Dorothy Sanders and James McKinney. The top of the page promised readers exclusive photographs and stories on the hostage crisis.

The lead stories on the front page were titled, **CAPTOR FEARED END OF WORLD** and **POLICE MAY HAVE BEEN LURED INTO AMBUSH.**

The January 13th, morning edition of the Commercial Appeal was highlighted with a picture of a TACT sniper inside the vacant Curry Ave. house. The front page headline was, **WAR OF NERVES CONTINUES AT HOUSE.** The two front page stories were grimly titled, **LONG VIGIL WEARS DOWN ONLOOKERS. FRUSTRATION AND TENSION MARK HOSTAGE SIEGE** and **OFFICER'S CAPTORS REFUSE TO EXPLAIN.**

The Commercial Appeal had already went to press with these stories even as the TACT unit stormed the house. A chronology of events was posted on page two along with a small story featuring Memphis Police Association President Maples apologizing for his criticism of the police administration.

"What we did was we overreacted without finding out the correct information before we made our statement. We were incorrect. We were wrong for doing that without finding out what was happening." Maples said.

Another small article on page two, titled **CAPTURED POLICEMAN'S RELATIVES WAIT SILENTLY**, gave a brief history of three officers, Hester, Turner and Schwill, and the emotional strain on the families of each.

The January 13th evening edition of the Press-Scimitar carried a caption on the very top of the front page, **SIEGE ON SHANNON STREET.** Below was the headline, **POLICE STORM HOUSE, KILL 7; TORTURED OFFICER FOUND DEAD.** Underneath the headline was a picture of ambulance attendants wheeling a body from the house.

Pictures of Sanders and Hester accompanied the story. Director Holt was quoted as saying that as early as the morning hours, of the 12th, it was suspected that Hester was being brutalized. Because it was believed, a pistol was being held to his head, the order to assault the house was not given.

"The order to assault the house, came only after it was felt, that Hester and perhaps others were already dead," Holt said.

Another article on the front page caused more than one police officer to shake their head in disbelief.

The article, with the title, **OFFICIALS FEARED HOME HELD DYNAMITE CACHE**, had Mayor Hackett, saying that officials were afraid that the hostage takers inside the house had dynamite. The Mayor alleged that at one point, during the siege, the suspects had said that they had a surprise, if officers tried to come inside.

Hackett said he had stayed all but one hour at the scene. He denied he ever took charge in the police operation or interfered in anyway.

"Since a city employee was in danger, I felt I needed to be there, to offer support," Hackett said.

In the coming days the Commercial Appeal flashed headlines and bylines throughout its paper, LEADER OF CULT MADE HIS OWN APOCALYPSE; HESTER DIED BEFORE RAID ON SHANNON; FUTILE HOPE DELAYED DEADLY ASSAULT; SCORES OF POLICEMEN WHO FLOCKED TO SIEGE SITE ADDED TO CONFUSION; DIRECTOR SAYS POLICE FEELING COMFORTABLE WITH SIEGE DISCLOSURE;

Incident Ranked Among Deadliest In Hostage Crises; Group Followed Bizarre Path to Doom; Mental Health Official Says Sanders Was Schizophrenic.

In a January 14th, article in the Commercial Appeal local black leaders lashed out at the police.

Maxine Smith, executive secretary of the N.A.A.C.P., told news affiliates that she was going to send off a telegram this afternoon to the U.S. Justice Department requesting they investigate the whole situation.

Walter Bailey, the county commissioner for the Hyde Park area, regretted what happened and said he was in no position to say if it could have been avoided. Bailey then added that he would have waited longer, whatever the required number of days, to avoid the killings.

Ray Maples, President of the Memphis Police Association, countered that the Justice Department needed to investigate whether Hester's civil rights had been violated.

"We're sick and tired when incidents like this occur and the first thing that we hear from knee-jerking liberals is that the officer did wrong. We're not just asking this locally, we're going nationally," Maples said.

In another article, an unnamed police officer was asked, just minutes after the siege ended, "where the operation had went wrong?"

His response was simple. "I'd say they messed up about 29 hours ago when he(Hester)was screaming for help and nobody came. If you were being beaten wouldn't you want somebody right away?"

The article went on to quote another officer who said that the TACT officers were begging to go in Tuesday night when Hester was seized. The officer went on to say, "They botched it bad. Somebody was afraid to make a decision."

In an unprecedented move, Director Holt held a press conference on January 18th and meticulously laid out everything the police department did during the siege. The conference lasted over two hours. The headline of **DRAMA, DESPAIR OF SIEGE REPLAYED** was accompanied by a photo of Holt and TACT commander Jim Music.

During the press conference, Holt assumed responsibility for the delay in assaulting the house and then the final decision in assaulting the house. He elaborated by saying he was backed up by over 250 years of police experience, meaning the exccutive command staff.

Holt described the TACT entry and the order in which the seven suspects died and which officer fired the probable fatal rounds. It was said that Watson shot and killed Lindberg Sanders and Thomas. Hubbard and Ray fired the rounds that killed Larnell Sanders, Harris and Jordan. After moving back through the house, Watson and Rutherford shot and killed Coleman and Summers killed Houston. Holt also told the media that it might take months before the ballistics tests came back.

"That's as close as we can reconstruct the sequence of events during the assault," Holt said.

Leaders in the black community were not satisfied with Holt's version of what had transpired.

"I think there are a number of bristling questions still unanswered, such as why couldn't the storming of the house been held off until the safety of everybody inside could be determined," County Commissioner Walter Bailey asked.

Bailey said he had a gut suspicion that the police may have been a bit heavy-handed.

Representative Harold Ford said he wanted to know who gave the order early on which prevented officers from entering the house to rescue Hester, whether it was given by Holt or Mayor Dick Hackett and whether inaction caused Hester's death.

"I don't feel that we have any more information to make a real assessment than we did at first," Maxine Smith, of the Memphis NAACP, said.

A protest march was staged by national, state and local officials from the Congress on Racial Equality. The sixty or so march-
ers rallied at City Hall to demand a complete explanation of the
deaths on Shannon Street.

Roy Innis, CORE national chairman said that a preliminary
investigation by CORE indicated that *eight people did not have to
die. Somebody wanted it to go down that way.*

The Commercial Appeal quoted Innis saying he was pleased
with the turnout but comments by Benjamin L. Hooks, NAACP
national executive director may have hindered that turnout.
Innis added that he was not criticizing Hooks for statements he
made on a news program that seemed to vindicate police.

"Hooks had probably been misinformed," Innis said.

In the Press-Scimitar Innis said that police tactics used to end
the siege were a way of regaining masculinity lost by having two
pistols taken away and an officer captured.

"That ego motivation led to the need for the assault," Innis
said.

A citizen's group headed by Nkechi Ajanaku announced it
would begin its own investigation into the death of the seven
black men killed on Shannon. Ajanaku said the group would
interview witnesses and gather information for a report that they
would issue in February. The group was sponsored by the Ben F.
Jones chapter of the National Bar Association.

In a Commercial Appeal article C. J. Morgan, the disc jockey
at WLOK, recounted his morning shows in late December. He
had talked daily of the pending lunar eclipse that was to take
place on December 30th, 1982. Because of volcanic ash in the air
astronomers were predicting a red moon.

"I always make a big deal out of lunar eclipses," Morgan said.

In mid January, in the midst of rumors that foretold additional police kidnapping, Police Director Holt publically denied

officers were refusing or avoiding patrolling certain areas of north Memphis. In the end, the rumors proved false.

On January 23, an entire page of the Commercial Appeal was devoted to letters to the editor on the Shannon Street affair.

My congratulations to you Memphis, you have really outdone anything I have seen before coming from California. When the house was stormed and all the occupants killed I first felt relieved to know that these sick fanatics would not be around to threaten us anymore. Instead of racial overtones this tragedy smacks of prejudice against the police. Imagine the public outcry that would have resulted if the police stood around outside and allowed a civilian to be tortured to death.

No one in his right mind could possible turn the brutal murder of Patrolman Hester into a racial issue, but it seems the black leaders of our city have done just that.

Many of us, both black and white are sick and tired of being subjected to some of the black community leader's attempts to lead us by our emotions into the racial injustice song and dance routine.

Justice has been served to those responsible and other criminal misfits should take notice.

I am black, so therefore I am not a racist. I feel that this situation was handled in the best way possible. As I watched the local news I witnessed a few black people making ridiculous remarks about Memphis policemen. I believe the shootings could have been avoided had the men been willing to cooperate with the policemen. It is not a matter of black and white, it's a matter of right and wrong. The seven men got what they deserved, because they didn't have to beat Patrolman Hester to a pulp.

It is unfortunate that our city is divided in the aftermath of the Shannon Avenue incident. At the same time many people must wonder what the reaction of Maxine Smith, Harold Ford, etc would have been had the murdered patrolman been black and the cult members white.

Mrs. Smith I believe you are guilty of racism. On the local news on Jan 13, you stated that you were very concerned about the facts surrounding the deaths of the seven black men on Shannon. Maybe it was a slip of the tongue or just perhaps you were not very concerned about the death of Patrolman Hester.

It is strange that I did not know Patrolman Hester, had probably never seen him, yet I feel that I have lost a dear friend.

CHAPTER 38
Funeral

January 15th, 1983
12:00 noon

T he officer found a parking spot a block away from the
church. As he reached into the back seat to collect his hat,
he wondered how long he could keep it together today.

It had been just over fifty-eight hours since he had watched
Hester's lifeless body being loaded into the back of the ambulance. He had driven home that day feeling strangely detached
emotionally from what he had experienced over the last two days.

He climbed into bed before 1pm on the 13th and despite the
whirl of sights and sounds that ebbed and flowed in his brain, he
fell immediately to sleep.

His wife came home a little after 4pm. Tires tracks across
her dormant mailbox flower bed and the odd angle his car was
parked across the drive-way told her all she needed to know. By
the back door stood his dirt stained boots. She never noticed the
boots had been removed without being untied.

She walked through the house and into the bedroom. Her
husband's uniform and leather goods lay piled up on the bedroom floor. She stared down at her sleeping husband. It was so

quiet in the bedroom; she shook her head as she bent down and picked up the clothes before quietly leaving the room. In ten years of marriage she could never remember a time when her husband had not snored.

He reached for his wife's hand as they walked towards the church. The muddy boots were now glistening with polish as they made their way slowly across the parking lot, the cold wind stinging his chapped face.

He had slept for over fifteen hours before waking. Several times during the night his wife had checked to see if he was still breathing. He had awakened around 3am on the 14th and after two tries was finally able to stand up. His aching knees and feet reminding him of the punishment he had put his body through.

He was sitting on the couch drinking coffee when his wife got up at 5am. She had found him staring out the window, totally absorbed in his thoughts. She had called out his name twice and touched him on the shoulder before he acknowledged her presence.

She walked through the living room several times as she got ready for work, each time her husband was staring blankly out the window. She walked over to kiss him on the cheek goodbye as she left for work and tasted the salt of tears that ran down his face. She said nothing about it and he never altered his gaze. They had found seats at the back of the church. She looked over at him as he flashed a quick smile and squeezed her hand. She could feel the tension in his body, while chords of somber music floated through the church.

Two white gloved officers, members of the honor guard, stood at attention at Hester's casket. Every fifteen minutes, two more officers walked to the casket to relieve the two standing post. All fifteen hundred seats in the church sanctuary were filled as the overflow of people stood in the lobby and along the back walls.

Flower arrangements and wreaths covered the podium and in the center a large yellow floral arrangement in the shape of a badge with the number 480 in the center.

Officers from Cincinnati, Ohio; Louisville, Kentucky; New York City, New York; Tulsa, Oklahoma and Orange County, California sat among officers from all across the southeastern part of the country.

To this day Memphis officers say it was the largest funeral they had ever attended.

Reverend Floyd Simmons had been Hester's pastor for twenty years at Elliston Baptist Church. He would preside now over the funeral, which had been moved to Eudora Baptist Church to allow for the large crowd. His words were gentle and comforting.

"When death came, happiness flooded his soul, remove the grief and celebrate the home going of Bobby. Open our eyes that we may behold the beauty of death."

North Precinct Inspector, James Ivy, had also spoke to those in attendance.

"Officer Hester was killed through no fault of his own and because of no action of his own but rather a lack of humility on the part of others," Ivy said.

When the fifty-five minute service came to a close, the pall bearers started down the center aisle. The church emptied as officers hurriedly lined up shoulder to shoulder on either side of the front doors. As the casket was brought out the doors it was followed by a solitary figure in full Scottish Highlander regalia. The solemn notes of *Amazing Grace* floated out into the parking lot as the command, ATTENTION, ORDER ARMS, brought all the gathered officers to full rigid attention as they saluted the passing casket.

He stood in the parking lot, his wife behind him, as he held the salute. The bitter cold was forgotten as tears rolled down his face. He felt his wife's hand lightly touch his back as his mind replayed the echoes of a pleading voice calling out into night.

The four hundred or so cars in the procession were escorted by motor officers from the Memphis Police Department and the Shelby County Sheriff's Office. The one mile plus procession began to slowly makes its way towards the cemetery.

People came out from businesses all along the route. Many holding American flags, while others saluted or doffed their caps. Traffic along the route came to a standstill as motorists pulled over and made the effort to get out of their cars as a sign of respect.

The drive to the grave site on Whitten Road, just north of I-40, would normally have taken ten minutes, but it would be two hours before every car had arrived and the grave side service began.

He had stopped crying as he drove silently in the procession. He felt his wife slowly patting his knee. He stared straight ahead, afraid to look towards her, knowing that if he did he would break down again.

The crowd waited silently as the casket was removed from the hearse. The command came again, ATTENTION, ORDER ARMS. In unison all officers saluted as the casket was placed under the canopy.

As the honor guard folded the American Flag that had laid draped over the coffin, Director Holt stepped forward and presented it to Anita Hester.

The TACT unit fired off a twenty-one gun salute followed by taps played by musician seaman Tracey Hooker and Memphis police officer Mark Collins.

Ray Schwill, against doctor's orders, had checked himself out of the hospital to attend the service. His left hand and arm were still heavily bandaged.

For the final time the order of ATTENTION was raised followed several seconds later by the call to OFFICERS IN RANK, DISMISSED.

Anita Hester was photographed clutching the American Flag. That picture, along with a photograph of the long procession would be on the front page of the Commercial Appeal the following day.

He walked slowly to the car his wife's arm wrapped around his waist. He didn't want to stand and commiserate with the other officers. The urge to get away from the sadness that surrounded the cemetery made him feel guilty. He didn't care, only one thought ran through his mind.

I just want to go home.

He hoped the echoes would one day fade away.

CHAPTER 39
Odd Assortment

I nvestigators had begun to assemble all the evidence that would be taken to the Tennessee Bureau of Investigation (TBI) Lab in Nashville, Tennessee.

Sergeant Landers obtained a blood and hair sample from Schwill, and blood samples from Turner, Aiken and Ray. The four officers had all received injuries, which led to some amount of blood loss within the house. The Medical Examiner's Office provided blood and hair samples from Hester's body and blood samples from all seven suspects.

The Medical Examiner's Office gave investigators bullet fragments recovered during the autopsies of the seven suspects. All clothing tagged at the city's property room and all items with blood on it were packaged up separately. All blood samples, obtained from within the house were picked up from U.T. College of Health Sciences, in Memphis.

January 30th, 1983

Sgt. Hammers and Hollie drove east on I-40 with eighty-one items of evidence. Three hours later they arrived at the TBI building.

Most of the items were traditional pieces of evidence needed for examination in any crime scene, such as the TACT team's M-16 rifles, the shotguns, and five .38 caliber revolvers.

Other stranger items included: A shirt pocket flap with M.P.A. stickpin, one M.P.D. name tag, R.S. Hester, a bloody pink pillow, a blue vest-bulletproof, one Vantage cigarette pack and one cigarette butt.

Memphis Investigators requested the following:
1. Each weapon be test fired in order to determine who fired the fatal rounds.
2. All items with blood be tested to determine whose blood was on what items.
3. Hair samples collected be compared to hair on the clothing of seven suspects, Schwill and Hester.

February 4th, 1983
   Dr. Harlan of the Medical Examiner's office notified the police department that Hester's blood work had come back and it indicated he had a blood alcohol level of 0.03 percent(ethyl alcohol). Harlan could offer no reason as to why Hester had alcohol in his system. He did offer a theory that Hester may have been given alcohol by those inside the house.

February 8th
   Lt. Tusant assigned Sgt. Wheeler and Officer Cooper to interview everyone Hester had been in contact with on the 11th of January to see if anyone had seen Hester drinking or appear to be under the influence of alcohol.

   Wheeler and Cooper got a copy of the log sheet for car 128 for the 11th and began the follow up with instructions to see if Hester or Schwill had been drinking alcohol while on duty.

Lt. Summers was interviewed and said he had been with the officers forty-five minutes before the Shannon Street call and had talked with them for half an hour and at no time detected the odor of alcohol or did either officer appear to be under the influence of alcohol.

Wheeler and Cooper went to 2327 Vandale and interviewed Diane Williams. Williams had talked to officers on a complaint call at her house. She said neither officer smelled of alcohol and both acted normal.

Cometrius Taylor, a distant relative of Lindberg's, who worked at Fast Service Gas Station and Drive-In Grocery at 2138 Chelsea told investigators she had known both officers for quite some time. She told investigators that her nicknames for Hester and Schwill, were "Smiley" and "Squeal".

They had been to the store on a complaint call and had stopped several other times during the night. Hester and Schwill had received the Shannon call while talking with her in the store. She said the officers acted normal and neither had been drinking.

Jacque Surratt, a waitress at the Southern Kitchen, said she knew the officers very well and that they had come in to eat the night of the 11th. She said she had never seen them drink and the business did not serve alcohol.

Sgt. Harker told investigators he had sat with Hester and Schwill on the 11th and neither officer had been drinking nor did he smell alcohol on them.

The investigation into the matter was closed.

June 28th, 1983

Almost six months to the day, Sgt. Hammers made the trip back to TBI and picked up all the items and a report which consisted of thirty typed pages signed by the Senior Serologist, Mike Martin; Senior Firearms Examiner L.A. Wilder; and Special Agent in Charge,

William Darby III.

The findings of T.B.I. were as follows:

Caucasian hairs found on the inside front door and love seat had the same microscopic characteristics as that of Hester. Caucasian hairs found in the clothing of Michael Coleman were dis-similar to hair from Schwill and Hester.

Caucasian hair found in the barrel of Hester's pistol, on the clothing of Andrew Houston and Earl Thomas were not adequate for significant comparison purposes.

Serological tests found human blood on numerous items of evidence and listed the blood types found which were compared to the blood types submitted by the police department.

Because several individuals had the same blood type it could not be conclusively shown whose blood was on what items of evidence. The test results could be used to show whose blood was not present on certain items.

The firearms identification tests were able to show the origin of spent .38 and .223 caliber casings that were recovered. All of the .223 fragments recovered from the bodies of the seven suspects were un-identifiable.

Four recovered spent bullets showed to be from Hester's pistol and six from Schwill's.

A bullet recovered from the body of Houston showed to have been fired from Lt. Summer's pistol while he had stood looking through the kitchen window.

None of the suspects had gunshot residue on their clothing.

After reviewing the TBI reports the department's investigation concluded its investigation on the ten officers who had fired shots while on the scene at Shannon Street.

Three officers (Norton, Hanscom, Aiken) and one Lieutenant (R.B. Summers), from the North Precinct, fired approximately 20 rounds from pistols and shotguns.

Six TACT officers (McNair, Watson, Summer, Rutherford, Ray, Hubbard) fired approximately 90 rounds from shotguns and M-16's.

The report read in part:

All ten of the police officers who fired their weapons did so in self-defense and/or to aid other officers who were being threatened with bodily harm by perpetrators inside 2239 Shannon.

The evidence collected and statements taken from the officers and citizens prove that the ten officers complied with the Memphis Police Department's Deadly Force Policy when they fired their weapons, thus all ten shootings in this case were ruled as being justified.

The guns were returned back to the officers or units they were assigned to. The remaining evidence was placed into standard white storage boxes, and placed on the floor of the property room at 201 Poplar. All the boxes and evidence envelopes bore the same writing. Case number 8301132672. R. Hester.

CHAPTER 40
Revisit

He has lain quiet for twenty-seven years in the far northeastern part of Forest Hill Cemetery East in a section appropriately named Garden of Peace. He is not alone, his father lays quietly in a grave beside him. Bobby's grave is marked with Hester in large eight inch block letters. On the upper left hand side in smaller letters reads Robert S., Born December 24th, 1948, Died January 13th, 1983. A small porcelain figurine of an angel sits on the right hand side.

He hurts no more, his soul has left this earth. He is the lucky one, for there are so many still here that carry the pain. A burden on their backs, a cross to bear. Officers who spoke about what happened told their stories with emotionless faces but their eyes told a far more hurtful saga.

Turner said he wished he had burst through the door with his gun in his hand instead of his night stick. Like most, Turner has relieved the event over and over again wondering what he could have done differently.

Davidson spoke softly of those thirty hours and his memories of hearing Hester being physically beaten and the screams that accompanied it. "Hard to listen to Hester screaming," Davidson said. After Shannon Street he would travel out of town on police association business and officers from other departments kept asking the same question, "Why didn't TACT go in sooner?" they would ask time after time.

Greg Hudgins spoke highly of Jim Wiechert and his performance that night. He remembered Wiechert staying on the radio for the majority of two days. Hudgins had stayed in communications till three or four in the morning on west radio then went home and drank whiskey sitting in front of the TV.

Ed Vidulich said what helped him get through those first few days was his work with the informant. "It kept me busy out picking people up, I didn't have time to sit around and get pissed off," Vidulich recounted. (A little over two years after speaking with Big Ed about Shannon Street he was murdered in his house. God Bless you Ed.)

Billy Robbins talks of the smells in the morgue and the unkempt condition of the seven suspects and how skinny they were. Like everyone else his memories seemed to be of yesterday, instead of two decades ago.

Wayne Hightower's memories are spoken in a whisper, with long pauses in between sentences. He stood on the school roof during his time there. He almost shuddered as he spoke of the terribly cold temperatures. As he told of seeing Hester's body for the first time, he was no longer standing on the roof of a parking garage at 201 Poplar in 2005 but rather as if he was in the funeral home and it was again 1983.

Kam Wong who was twenty-one years old in 1983, remembers leaving their store on Chelsea on the night of January 11th with his family. They had driven the normal route home, north on Hyde Park, east of Shannon to Hollywood, then north to the interstate. They had passed 2239 Shannon at around 8:30pm.

Tim Helldorfer, like Hudgins, remembers Wiechert's calm voice on the air punctuated by the shrill ravings of Lindberg. He still speaks with great admiration for Chief Moore.

Russ Aikens told the author that after being relieved from his post at the corner of the house on the 11th he had noticed his wedding band was missing. Crime Scene officers located the ring on the 13th inside the house. The ring had a small indentation in it from a bullet strike.

So many unanswered questions swirl around what took place twenty-seven years ago. A vast amount of information was collected from this one event. There is so much information yet so few answers as to why this happened.

Did the police spark the incident with a simple phone call or by showing up at 2239 Shannon?

Is a police officer, with what one member of the religious group termed a bad attitude, reason to assault officers and beat another officer to death?

The majority of the men who were in the house gave statements placing the blame on Lindberg or Coleman rather than the police.

Was it a set up as some officer's feel?

What justification could there ever be for anyone to beat a human being to death over a six to ten hour period?

What are the rules for hostage negotiations?

What are the rules when the hostage is being beaten?

Who made the decisions and why were they made?

Were there some in the house that wanted to surrender?

If someone wanted to surrender why didn't they leave over the course of the thirty hour siege?

Did Lindberg really have that much control over those inside?

What went on inside the house for thirty hours?

A chain of trivial events that fell into place and ended in tragedy for so very many people. Never has one event in the history of the Memphis Police Department caused as much turmoil as Shannon Street. The debate among those that were there as to why it happened is still as heated as it was back then.

Many officers are still bitter about the outcome and how it was handled. Some officers spoke with open contempt towards other officers on the scene for perceived acts of cowardice.

Like the Kennedy Assassination, every officer on the job then, can tell you what he or she was doing on January 11th, 1983.

For those who were there, life carried on but each one left a little bit of themselves there.

A member of the TACT unit during the siege, Godwin, became the Director of Police Services in Memphis in 2004. Schwill rose to the rank of Deputy Director before retiring in 2004. Turner became the President of the Memphis Police Association. Aiken served as his Vice-President and Robbins the Secretary-Treasurer. Hightower rose to the rank of Lieutenant and served for many years in the Robbery Bureau. Mhoon became a Major in Uniform Patrol. Oliver became a Major. Ross, Vidulich, Pfaffenroth, Chalk and Wong became Lieutenants.

Hanscom retired as a thirty year Captain. Downen and Pugh retired as a Majors. Pugh's son, Matt, graduated from the police academy with the author in 1990.

Davidson made Sergeant and worked in Robbery before retiring. McWilliams made Sergeant and retired from the Homicide Bureau. Helldorfer later served on the TACT unit and after making Sergeant worked in Homicide. Tusant became a Deputy Chief in 2004. The Superintendent of Memphis City Schools at the time, Willie Herenton, would later become the mayor of Memphis, unseating Hackett.

What of the TACT unit, that group of professionals, that one politician would later malign as a bunch of hired killers. Their story as well as the siege did not end on January 13th, 1983.

In January of 1983 the Justice Department began an investigation into allegations of possible police mis-conduct. This investigation was widened in early February to include any violations of federal law. The probe would include any violations of the civil rights of Schwill and Hester.

John Wilson, a Justice Department assistant director of public affairs was asked if the expanded probe would include whether there had been a violation of the civil rights of the two officers. "Well, a police officer died," Wilson said without elaborating.

In January of 1984 families of the seven suspects filed a federal civil lawsuit asking for 17.5 million dollars. The suit, in part said the killings were unwarranted, cruel, inhuman, unjustifiable and involved the excessive use of force under the circumstances.

The defendants in the case were Mayor Hackett, Director Holt, TACT commander Jim Music, Ray Schwill and the six TACT officers on the primary assault team.

An attorney representing the families said the incident was a gross use of excessive force by the police department. Sanders and the others were found guilty and executed on the scene for Hester's death.

The attorney claimed the police knew Sanders was mentally ill but turned down an offer of help from Sanders physician.

In November of 1984 the Justice Department announced they had found no criminal violations in their investigation.

Maxine Smith of the Memphis Chapter of the NAACP said she was dismayed. "A great injustice has been rendered." She went on to say that, "As we look at the racism that pervades this country and particularly this administration we should not be surprised." "Our top lawmaking officials have no concern for the rights and protection of black citizens."

An attorney representing the suspect's families said the Justice Department findings would have no bearing on the civil lawsuit.

Shortly after the Justice Department investigation concluded in November of 1984 a reporter for the Commercial Appeal asked Director Holt for a copy of the official report that had been sent to the Justice Department. Holt refused the request. The Commercial Appeal sued the department for access to all the records pertaining to the case under the state of Tennessee's open records law.

Echoes of Shannon Street

Chancellor Alissandratos, in December of 1984 sided with the Commercial Appeal. The city appealed the ruling and the state Court of Appeals, in a 2 to 1 decision, in August of 1985

denied the city of Memphis' appeal and ordered the records be made available. The city again appealed and the State Supreme Court, in May of 1986, also denied the appeal and ordered the records turned over to the newspaper.

In 1990 with the civil lawsuit still pending in Federal Court attorney's for the families located a witness.

William Burt gave a sworn statement as to what he saw when the TACT unit entered the house. His statement differed greatly from the officer's statements.

Burt, who was living at 2242 Curry at the time of the incident said he was looking out his back window that morning when the TACT officers were at the back door of Sanders' house. Three men walked out of the back door of the house with their hands up trying to surrender. According to Burt, officers pushed the three men back into the house.

By 1995 the civil case had run its course with no money being awarded to the families and the TACT unit cleared of any wrong doing.

In 2005, Paulette Sutton, the U.T. Medical blood expert, told the author about her feelings.

"We did our jobs and did them well, but it would have been nice to just leave and forget everything that had happened. As scientists, we must be objective or we wouldn't be good at our work. The problem is that, in order to do this for very long, you have to care. Once the job is done, the scientific objectivity can be put away but the memories must then be handled."

Maybe Ms. Sutton's words speak not just for the civilian experts who ventured to that house. There are a lot of police officers who wish the very same sentiments.

A thousand page investigation of a single event, a single tragedy. If time does truly heal all wounds, then it may take another twenty years for the healing process to be completed on this story.

The echoes that sounded so long ago still linger in the air, still ring in the ears of those who were there.

James R. Howell

James is a 1984 graduate of Austin Peay State University with a B.S. Degree in History. He has been employed with the State of Tennessee as a Park Ranger; an Officer with the United States Secret Service and since 1990 has been an Officer with the Memphis Police Department where he has risen to the rank of Major.

Acknowledgments

As always I thank my wife Dana and my family for their support in my continuing quest to rise above mediocrity. My heartfelt thanks to Kelly Nichols for helping to make this book a reality. The countless hours she spent teaching an old man how writing a book, is really done, was most certainly a debt I will never be able to repay. She is probably as glad as I am the book is finished, as she most certainly deserves a rest. Thanks to Paulette Sutton whose expertise in the field of blood is awe inspiring. I had the pleasure of seeing Ms. Sutton at work on several homicide scenes. She is amazing. To Ed Vidulich, Tommy Turner, Russ Aiken, Ronnie McWilliams, Wayne Hightower, Don Ross, Greg Hudgins and Mike Davidson and the unnamed officers who all took time to talk with me. Their pain was real and I do certainly appreciate not only their memories but their support to this project. Special kudos to Tim Helldorfer for help in tracking down some of the officers involved your expertly drawn map of the old police building and for your help along with Ben Pruitt in answering countless questions about the inner workings of the TACT unit and its operations. Thanks to Mark Pfaffenroth and Jeff Larkin, who negotiated at both St. Jude and Shannon Street, for all their help. Thanks to Kam Wong and Charlie Gordon for all their invaluable info on people and places in the north precinct and specifically Hyde Park. Thanks a bunch to Karen Schaber for her photo expertise and assistance and to Cody Wilkerson who helped in compiling the case file.

Made in the USA
Lexington, KY
27 January 2014